Gertrud Orff

Key Concepts in the Orff Music Therapy

Gertrud Orff, born in Munich, undertook General Music and Composition studies with Carl Orff. From 1949 to 1953 she was a collaborator
in the Orff-Schulwerk editions and from 1961 to 1966 she taught music
in elementary schools. She was the Orff-Schulwerk specialist in the
Bellflower Project 'Creativity and Participation in Music Education',
California from 1966 to 1969 and held seminars in various colleges and
universities in the United States between 1966 and 1974. Since 1970
she has been developing the 'Orff-Musiktherapie' at the 'Kinderzen-
trum und Forschungsstelle für Soziale Pädiatrie und Jugendmedizin
der Universität München' and has held seminars for music therapy
throughout Europe.

By the same author

The Orff Music Therapy
ED 11427   Schott London

Front cover photo: Peter Vocke
(The subject is a two-year-old girl of retarded development
unable as yet to speak, stand or walk.)

Gertrud Orff

Key Concepts in the Orff Music Therapy

Definitions and Examples

Translated from the German
by Jeremy Day and Shirley Salmon

SCHOTT

ED 12339

London · Mainz · New York · Tokyo

Sources

Bettelheim, B.	*The Empty Fortresss: infantile autism and the birth of the self.* New York, 1967. London, 1968
	Die Geburt des Selbst. (Translation) Munich, 1977
Burkhardt, C.J.	Burkhardt-Rychner Letters. Frankfurt, 1970
Buytendijk, F.J.J.	*Zur Phänomenologie der Begegnung.* Eranos Yearbook 1950. Zürich
Cage, J.	*Silence* (essays and lectures). Middletown, Connecticut, 1961
Camus, A.	*Noces.* Paris, 1950
Flitner, A.	*Das Kinderspiel.* Munich, 1976
Heidegger, M.	*Sein und Zeit.* Tübingen, 1949
	Being and Time. (Translated by J. Macquarrie and E. Robinson) Oxford, 1962
Huizinga, J.	*Homo ludens. A Study of the play-element in culture.* (Translated by R.F.C. Hull) London, 1949
McLuhan, M.	*Understanding Media: the extensions of man.* London, 1964
Neumann, E.	Eranos Yearbook 1951. Zürich
Novalis	*Fragmente.*
Piaget, J.	Complete works.
Plato	Complete works.
Portmann, A.	*Das Spiel als gestaltete Zeit.* Munich, 1976
Saint-Exupéry, A. de	*Pilot de guerre.* Paris, 1942
	Flight to Arras. (Translated by L. Galantière) London, 1942
Saint-Exupéry, A. de	*Lettre à un Otage.* Paris, 1944
Saint-Exupéry, A. de	*Citadelle.* Paris, 1948
Spitz, R.	*Vom Dialog.* Stuttgart, 1976

(English translations have been given where available)

First published in German under the title
Schlüsselbegriffe der Orff-Musiktherapie
© 1984 Psychologie Verlags Union, GmbH

English translation:
© 1989 Schott & Co. Ltd, London

British Library Cataloguing in Publication Data

Orff, Gertrud
   Key concepts in the Orff music therapy:
   definitions and examples. [Schlüsselbegriffe
   der Orff-Musiktherapie]
   1. Handicapped children. Music therapy
   I. Schlüsselbegriffe der Orff-Musiktherapie
   II. Title
   615.8'51554

   ISBN 0-946535-10-8

ED 12339

Contents

Introduction

The present book contains 77 concepts that, in the course of more than ten years' empirical work as a music therapist, have proved to be of fundamental importance in:

- 'placing' a child: his diagnosis
- further developing his existing abilities: his prognosis
- tackling his abnormality: his therapy

Such a concept provides a tangible link to the condition being considered. We can talk about it – we have a terminology to work with.

Music therapy itself is still for many people a subject of hot debate. One often hears: 'Well, after all, music says "something" to everybody', but exactly what effects it can have and how these can be put to practical use is often unclear.

These key concepts are mainly intended for those who work with difficult children – therapists, teachers, psychologists – all those explorers in this field wanting to analyse and understand the development of a therapy and make its possible uses available to others.

At the beginning of my work as a music therapist, the first two concepts I considered to be 'key' were 'initiative' and 'imitation': did a particular child's behaviour tend more towards the initiative or imitative side? A further concept was 'emotion': does the child show any at all? Does he show too much, or too little? Further, does the child show aggressiveness, and if so, why? What are the reasons for his stereotype behaviour? Using such concepts I tried to approach a child by means of an objective understanding of his condition.

Apropos the word 'key'. A key alone has no significance; it presupposes a lock, and its function is to unlock, to open – or to close.

The word 'key' can be found time and again in verse and song:
. . . verloren ist das sluezzelin . . . , I haven't got the key . . .

Lock the dairy door	Je vais à la noce,
lock the dairy door,	ma clef dans ma poche,
chickle, chakle chee,	ma poche est percée,
I haven't got the key.	j'ai perdu ma clef.

A lock is the given condition, we bring the key to it and unlock it, but we keep the key with us. Only rarely do we find a lock and its key together. Furthermore, there are plenty of keys but only one for a particular lock, the one that was made for it.

A word 'dropped' by a child during a therapy session can often turn out to be a key that the therapist should definitely pick up! In this way the first, whispered but still intelligible, sentence spoken by Antonia, a four-year-old blind girl, opened up quite unexpected areas of common experience for the session. The therapist had spotted the key and taken it up, and a whole string of keys was the result! – 'that's a carpet.'

A child in need of therapy consists of a whole complex of character-istics. Any disturbance or handicap is unlikely to be present in an uncomplicated, 'pure' form.

In one or other of the children cited in my examples the reader will perhaps recognize children they themselves have worked with or still have in therapy. I enjoy being a music therapist and believe, along with Novalis, that 'where there are children, there's the Golden Age!'

Gertrud Orff

All my examples are from music therapy sessions at the Kinderzen-trum in Munich headed by Prof. Dr. Theodor Hellbrügge. I have him to thank for making possible this fascinating work at his institute.

References in the text to the Orff Music Therapy (Orff Musiktherapie) are to the translation by Margaret Murray published by Schott & Co. Ltd, London (ED 11427). The abbreviation OMT is used throughout.

I Perception

1

Perception: comprehension of 'reality', of events, of things around one. We can distinguish between two ways of perceiving:

– to *observe*, to *discern* implies a striving towards comprehension; an active process.

– to *apprehend*, to *become aware of* is a more passive process. It implies a receptivity, a pregnant readiness to absorb phenomena.

Perception manifests itself in reactions and counter-reactions to somebody or something. This 'turning towards' a person or thing is the goal of any therapeutic activity.

To apprehend does not mean to analyse, nor does it mean to understand. It requires gaining access to a spectacle and taking part in that spectacle.

Antoine de Saint-Exupéry

In Music Therapy:

Perception is the *conditio sine qua non* in music therapy. Nothing is possible without it. We distinguish between such awareness on an acoustic, a tactile, an optical and a social level. These various levels are likely to be developed to a different extent in each child in need of therapy. In cases where such children's perceptive abilities are normal, problems will be found in their behaviour, their concentration or their social co-operation. Quite dramatic deficiencies in visual perception are possible in normal-sighted children, especially in cases of severe deprivation. The optic angle (normally more than 180 degrees) can be reduced to as little as 40 degrees. The child can take in only what is directly in front of him and not more than half an arm's length away. His world stops there.

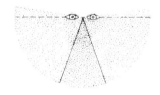

We can achieve a widening of the optic angle via the child's acoustic perception. His facial expression and his mien (see No.2) tell us that he has heard a tone, played, say, on a large cymbal held in front of him. This tone should by no means take him by surprise. It should be pleasantly resonant, designed to fascinate. If the therapist keeps repeating the tone, now a little to the left now to the right, the child's eyes will follow the sound. Played above or behind him the tone will stimulate the child to raise or lower his head or perhaps even to turn his head and body. Musical sounds are ideally suited for provoking a reaction and the optimal use of them therapeutically can lead to a successful break-through even in severe cases of perceptive disturbance.

Perception, bodily movement and emotion (inner agitation) are all intimately related. Each one affects and determines the others.

9

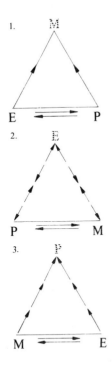

To describe this process we could imagine a triangle whose points represent the three concepts perception, movement and emotion. Stimulation of any one of these points charges a current that inevitably energizes the others. The music therapist tries to achieve the all-important initial induction by acoustic means. Once the circuit has been broken into, mutual stimulation between the three conditions is possible. Any one of these three might, as yet, be under-developed or lacking:

1. **Movement**
   Any impairment here may be coupled with speech problems. Therefore, improvement achieved via perception and emotion can also have a positive influence on speech (see **Movement** – No.20).

2. **Emotion**
   With non-verbal children (mutism), autistic children or in cases of deprivation, movement and perception are usually present but lack sufficient dynamism to affect emotion. Their efforts repeatedly fall short of the mark (see **Emotion** – No.4).

3. **Perception**
   This can be lacking with the severely mentally handicapped. Movement is relatively well-developed and emotional activity is clearly evident, but there is no integration through perceptive awareness. The movements are constant but purposeless. The child is hyper-active and easily distracted.

In cases where a defence against perception is set up, as in children with autistic tendencies, perception, both optical and acoustic, often does in fact take place but much more quickly than expected. And, because the child immediately afterwards shuts himself off again, the therapist may not even have noticed. The child rejects all further approaches, and repeated attempts to establish contact again serve only to strengthen his isolation. The only possibility left open to the therapist is to surprise the child. Any reactions may not immediately be apparent but an observant therapist will eventually be able to come to a confident diagnosis: *perception* has taken place but *contact* is refused.

The therapist is under the same obligation to develop his own perceptive abilities. The abilities to observe clearly and retain details until they can be documented are essential. Audio and video recordings are a useful aid but they are not always available, neither is their use always appropriate. *Our work demands from the therapist a benign attentiveness at all times during the therapy.*

2

Mien: outward expression (facial expression, bearing, body language) of inner feelings, mood or character. Control is possible and one can stop one's feeling breaking to the surface (not 'betray' oneself), but to present convincingly feelings or characteristics that are not genuine is difficult.

In Music Therapy:

The child's mien is of key importance in the therapy. When he cannot speak or refuses to, it provides a point of contact for the therapist. Control over mien is above all exercised by the autistic child.

3

Eye-contact: deliberate and direct eye-to-eye communication between two people. A non-verbal expression of endorsement, inquiry, agreement. Can range in intensity from the superficial to the profound.

In Music Therapy:

Eye-contact is an important factor in the therapy: does it take place? and if so, does it happen as a matter of course? – does the initiative come from the child? or does the child, in fact, try to avoid it? – or is it the only thing the child wants? (a child does nothing but stare into the therapist's eyes).

A good deal of strength is required to withstand the currents created by such eye-contact. Under some circumstances this can be too much for a child and he will not risk it. Any attempt to induce contact would be wrong. It will occur when the child feels strong enough.

On the other hand, the therapist may notice out of the corner of his eye that a child wants to establish eye-contact. He may decide not to return this look immediately. In this case his intention would be to encourage and strengthen the child's attentiveness.

Blind children have their own form of 'eye-contact', namely echolalia. A need for reassurance causes them to repeat themselves and what is said to them. This can lead to a faulty diagnosis of their condition, or to a bad prognosis of their mental capabilities. The blind child's echolalia, at first a necessity for him, later used almost playfully, will eventually change unexpectedly into an ability to converse normally.

4

Emotion: state of feeling, degree of agitation or excitement. An external stimulus penetrates the organism and transforms the existing emotional state, intensifies or diminishes the degree of inner commotion.

Human emotion is a mode of existence.

F.J.J. Buytendijk

In Music Therapy:

Therapeutic work can only be carried out effectively in an atmosphere of charged emotions. It is the therapist's task to bring about this condition. His observations help him determine which stimuli (musical sounds, rhythms, words, gestures) would be appropriate;

also how and to what extent they should be used (the 'dose', see No.11). What makes therapeutic intervention possible and effective is the flexibility of a child's emotional state which can be heightened, irritated or even obstructed as necessary. Music will normally have the effect of heightening the emotions. Where this would be inappropriate (with the severely mentally handicapped for example) then a measure of multi-sensory techniques within the context of music therapy can help.

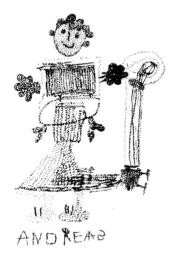

AND REAS

5

Fascination: consciously or not the therapist is always trying to awaken what is effectively the driving force behind perception – fascination. This can both broaden and concentrate a child's horizons; it heightens, consolidates, lays bare. *Fascination produces emotive behaviour and this opening up of the emotional state of the child makes therapeutic work possible.*

In Music Therapy:

A rhythm, a song or a melody are all essentially fascination in concrete form. The therapist should introduce them with charged (but not exaggerated or over-enthusiastic) dynamism: the child looks and listens, takes part in the proceedings – through *fascination becomes captivated*. The atmosphere must remain natural and down-to-earth at all times; any 'over-acting' by the therapist would only have a negative therapeutic effect. Fascination puts the child into a 'pretend' state of mind, he becomes part of the game or show. A fertile imagination grows out of the fascination which, after an initial spark from the therapist, kindles a creative life of its own (see **Cantus-memoria-meditatio** – No.76).

6

Elevation: – a higher form of fascination. The relatively static condition, fascination, raised to a more dynamic level. It occurs during intensive play. A child's involvement in the music being played is so intense that he 'loses' himself within the group. Elevation promotes group awareness and is socially binding. Therapeutically it is an important factor but potentially dangerous because work can easily be disrupted either from within or outside the group.

7

Imitation: plays a large part in musical training – repeating (singing or playing) the same melody, playing an answering phrase in the same style and so on. As repetition is a vital principle in music, so we can say that imitation is an organic part of our work with music.

In Music Therapy:

Simply training children to imitate perfectly is not our aim as this can only destroy their individual initiative. *Imitation should always be an active process understood as a game by the children.* Wherever the child's handicap permits (where he is able to express himself) the therapist should initially repeat something the child has done, showing it to him again, making him more aware of it – also of any stereotyped actions. Such imitation exercises should always be a lively two-way process that is also fun for the child when he 'catches on'. With the severely mentally handicapped short imitative repetitions that have been understood are worth more than longer passages that have been learnt by heart.

8

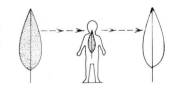

Secondary imitation: a concept developed in the OMT from the original meaning of the Latin word 'imitari'. One meaning of the word is imitation as we understand it. Another meaning, however, is to present something that did not previously exist, to reveal something new, disclose something. A late flowering so to speak, 'delayed' imitation.

In Music Therapy:

Something a child has heard time and again, and which he has imitated as well perhaps, becomes a part of him, is stored away and nurtured until it one day re-emerges in a new and unexpected form. We learn to speak in just this way too, not by continued repetition but by a constant exposure to the wealth of language. Repetitions in the course of the therapy must be in this sense – of providing 'food for thought' – and not in the sense of requiring the child to 'do it exactly as I do' (see **Trust** – No. 47, **Time** – No. 51, **Patience** – No. 69 and **Therapist** – No. 75).

9

Impulse: the sound and rhythm of the word itself, 'pulse'. An impulse sparks off something that did not exist before. An impulse is new every time; life and movement live from impulses; impulses, themselves intangible, manifest themselves in something concrete.

In Music Therapy:

An impulse is the most important active agent in the therapy. It is often impossible to predict which impulse will bring about a particular movement, musical tone, thought, glance or sigh. Well-directed impulses are sometimes possible if one has already seen that this or that impulse in a particular situation has a particular effect; but ultimately one can only hope that the same effect is sparked off a second time! A child's reaction, brought about by the therapist, can in turn become an impulse for the therapist himself. *In this way impulses are exchanged in the group, the one activating the next.* An impulse is often the result of a well-administered amount ('dose') of *provocation*.

The origin of the word 'impulse' is the Latin 'impello', meaning to strike against, to touch something with a stroke. This is exactly what we do to our instruments (xylophones, drums, cymbals, *etc.*) to make them resound. Whoever strikes an instrument sets up a chain reaction of resonance that includes himself. For this reason it is so important that the initial impulse to strike an instrument should come from the child. If the child is not able to move independently and the therapist senses that he wants to play on an instrument, then the therapist becomes the agent of the child's impulse, in that he holds the beaters with or for him.

10

Repetition: promotes the learning process and the patience and receptiveness that are a necessary part of it. Music is to a great extent built on the principle of repetition. As in this simple song, for example:

1. Es war eine Mutter, die hatte vier Kinder,
   den Frühling, den Sommer, den Herbst und den Winter.
2. Der Frühling bringt Blumen, der Sommer den Klee,
   der Herbst der bringt Trauben, der Winter den Schnee.

1. There once was a mother, and she had four children,
   the spring-time, the summer, the autumn and winter.
2. The spring-time brings flowers, the summer brings clover,
   the autumn brings grapes and the winter brings snow.

The two half-lines consist of exactly the same melody with a rhythm of regular crotchets throughout. It is the text that provides the structure just as the intervals make a melody out of the crotchets which would otherwise simply form a continuous ostinato.

In Music Therapy:

Such an economical form as in the previous example (and the more economical a melody is, the better it is) leaves freedom for emotional experience. The melody is easily learnt, each new verse drives it home, and one is soon an active participant. The way is open for individual expression or observation of the others in the group. Pressure-free group activity! What tension there is (and any emotional involvement implies tension) is within the context of there being no pressure to succeed. This is why stutterers do not stutter when they are singing.

Paradox: the structure of a melody permits a freedom of expression typical of unstructured activities.

The rhymes in the previous example, one in each verse (Kinder-Winter, Klee-Schnee), make it easier to remember the song and maintain the relaxed atmosphere.

The *Rondo* form (where the recurring main tune is played by everybody while each plays his solo in between) also provides an opportunity for work with repetition.

11

Dose: the amount of something offered or administered.

In Music Therapy:

Whatever the therapist offers a particular child or group, it is important for him to decide how much and exactly when it should be brought into play in order to develop or maintain a particular situation. In the use of provocation, censure or attention, or when the therapist occasionally decides he should ignore a child, the correct dose is especially important. *Exactly what should be administered will be determined according to the ISO-Principle* (see No.67). The more the therapist becomes aware of the probable results of a particular treatment the easier it will become for him to judge the correct dose.

12

Memory: can retain more easily what has been directly experienced. Music helps a) because the child takes an active part, and b) by making possible repetitive work that need never be monotonous. Lively alterations in the delivery (louder, quieter, one child alone, the whole group) bring variety; structural changes (variations) make a piece new every time. Concentrated work can result in the improvement of a child's alertness, an essential component in memory-training.

In Music Therapy:

Because the memory works most effectively with personal experiences, it is the initial confrontation with something that is the most significant. This should be striking, a tangible impulse for future reference. A single word (whether from the therapist or from the child) is often enough to register an experience, and a simple repetition of that word recreates the whole experience. One word can be the password to large areas of memory.

For this reason exclusively non-verbal communication in therapy with children will have a negative, if not paralysing, effect on the memory in the long run. Words and concepts have the power to electrify.

II Provocation

13

Provocation: in the sense of to rouse, to stimulate and not to aggravate or intimidate, is an important therapeutic means. It should introduce a stimulus that holds a child's interest, expands and enriches his comprehension. After repeated use any stimulus will lose its effectiveness, its 'edge'. A new stimulus is a new provocation, a challenge to the child to extend his capacities. *Provocation is an element in any growth process.* Correctly used it promotes growth from the inside making the results visible in the child's behaviour.

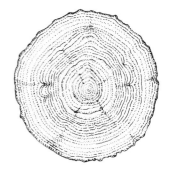

In Music Therapy:

Provocation is not necessary and should not be used where perception and impulses are obviously present and active. Provocation can then only disrupt and will have a negative effect. Provocation is necessary again to bring new life into a well-practised routine that has lost its dynamism.

14

Stimulus: arousal to activity or energy. The German word 'Reiz' is more complex, meaning any attack on a closed surface both figuratively and literally (an irritation to the skin, for example). The word has an aggressive sound too (pronounced 'rei*tz*') and means literally 'to tear oneself apart, break out of oneself'.

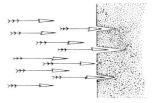

In Music Therapy:

Sounds can be a stimulus as long as acoustic perception takes place. In a multi-sensory context, optical stimuli or those arising out of a particular situation are possible. The surroundings should be stimulating. Over-stimulation loses its stimulating effect. The amount ('dose') and the quality of a stimulus determine its effectiveness.

No movement without solicitation.

Novalis

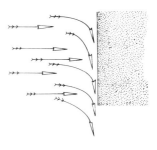

15

Threshold of sensitivity: a neurological concept. The location in the brain that controls the entry of stimuli. It acts as a guard and protector, in other words not everything is allowed in. It must first be sufficiently stimulated.

In Music Therapy:

In his confrontation with the threshold of sensitivity, which stimulus (and in what strength) will gain access is something the therapist's experience must tell him. He soon learns that an acoustic stimulus will not necessarily be more effective if played louder and that music alone is not always the ideal medium. A child can resist this stimulus as any other.

16

Suspense: an exceptional condition that is usually followed by a relaxation of tension. A normal, stable condition lies somewhere in between – until it once more fluctuates up or down (see **Elevation –** No.6).

In Music Therapy:

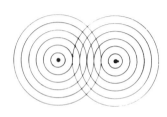

A state of suspense should materialize during music therapy. It is possible between a child and the instrument, the activity, or others in the group. In this condition the senses are alert, the consciousness awake and receptive. An ideal state of suspense, however, one that is neither over-tense nor short-lived, is difficult to establish. Suspense is the charged space between two poles, mental motoric so to speak. A well-balanced condition can also benefit the actual motor development.

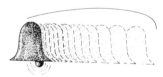

Inevitably, when one creates a sound on an instument one has previously *wanted* to do it. This is the initial suspense between player and instrument. The sound itself leads to suspense between it and the player who is now a listening bystander. This becomes most relevant with long-lasting sounds such as those made on a large cymbal or a gong. Some children will listen to the sound until it has faded away completely and only then play another note. A relationship with the instrument is established which, if it occurs with an autistic child, is a hopeful sign and can be the beginning of social contact.

If such a resonant instrument is struck endlessly without interruption it suggests motor impulses without the corresponding beneficial suspense between player and instrument. The therapist will exchange the instrument for one with short-lived sounds as quickly as possible. A correct state of suspense between player and instrument results in a style of playing appropriate to the instrument. This can also stimulate verbal expression. First of all, though, the instrument can be a means of relieving tension, of letting off steam. In loud, vigorous play the instrument becomes the child's partner and opponent, something to get to know and come to terms with (see **Practice** – No.31). The possibility exists that the child will learn to view his own way of playing objectively and this non-verbal communication with himself, manifested concretely in the sounds

18

produced, is of great therapeutic significance. The state of suspense within a particular child finds expression in the speed with which he plays naturally, his natural rhythm.

Example: A blind girl's natural rhythm was very slow, only about 80 strokes a minute. Her manner was accordingly very sluggish, she hardly stirred at all and she would keep repeating the stereotype question 'what's that?' The question was always willingly answered, even repeatedly, and everything revolved around this single initiative, this apparent interest. The girl exploited this situation to avoid greater demands on her and her progress was inevitably slow. An illness had left her blind at the age of two and now at five she was putting it to good use for an easy, untroubled life. She gave herself away one day when she said 'that's a bird!' She had bypassed her own stereotype question. The musical sounds around her had exposed her emotional state to the extent that she could make a direct statement. I asked her where she saw a bird, whereupon she went to a tapestry on the wall and pointed to a highly stylized representation of a bird woven into the fabric. It was astonishing but she had seen and recognized something at a distance of ten feet or so. (A medical examination also discovered an improvement in her sight, something the parents chose to ignore however, through their inability to adapt to a new, more relevant form of treatment.) Having betrayed her true condition she became obstinate, developed behavioural problems, refused to co-operate and did everything she could to parry all demands made on her. Eventually she was unable to resist reacting to this or that stimulus and would occasionally respond to a challenge to take part. Her natural rhythm, her musical 'pulse', increased in speed to about 120, which may be considered normal.

Quite the opposite was the case with a severely disturbed boy who did not speak. His 'pulse' was as high as 360 strokes a minute and the strokes were aggressive and loud. With this style of playing he cut himself off completely from any group work – it was as if he was erecting a wall around himself with it – and the deluge of sound was often frightening.

17

Challenge: a challenge (or invitation or demand) to do something is usually understood as coming from the therapist but a challenge from the child to the therapist is also important!

In Music Therapy:

We distinguish between a verbal and non-verbal challenge. Non-verbal challenges are especially important with children capable of speech. Non-verbal children, whether the condition is permanent or only passing, require challenges supported by language. Challenges made to hearing-impaired children should be put into words as well in order to develop their comprehension of language.

We interpret negatively a child's failure to respond to a challenge but do we always respond to his challenges? Is it even always possible to respond adequately? Failure to take up a challenge can mean:

1. that I don't want to
2. that I'm unable to
3. that I'm so preoccupied with something else that I haven't noticed!

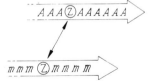

For the therapist, timing is critical but it is difficult always to judge the right moment to introduce a challenge. Any therapist who is aware of how carefully he must approach the question of challenging a child will first examine his own approach critically. Video recordings are useful: how do I behave? Am I too eager, do I push too hard, do I observe carefully enough, do I give too little? Critical self-examination: do I, verbally or with a look, offer too much reassurance or too little? We must all work on our weak points. We must become aware of the whole palette of possibilities involved in a challenge right down to the importance of the tone of voice we use.

18

Over-challenging: too much is demanded of the child too soon.

In Music Therapy:

Over-challenging a child, making excessive demands on him, is harmful. Instead of keeping to the child's pace the therapist wants too much. At this point children stop reacting to the therapist, group dynamism is lost, and the result is either unproductive chaos or everybody simply 'switches off'. The music therapist who has studied music or trained to be a musician tends to over-emphasize the musical side. Children's understanding of music is different however. For them it is much more a question of self-expression. Up to about the age of five, pre-melodic (see No.35) and pre-rhythmic (see No.33) musical expression is relevant. With a handicapped child the age will be higher. The time will come eventually when melodic work becomes important and intelligible to the child.

19

Under-challenging: the child's capacity is underestimated, too little is demanded or the challenges are always the same.

In Music Therapy:

This has an equally detrimental effect on the individual and the group as over-challenging. Chaos is again the result – aggressive behaviour and a destructive attitude towards instruments and apparatus. The 'barometer' of a session should not register dramatically different readings. Whether the atmosphere is calm or stormy it should be allowed to continue in the same vein (see **ISO-Principle** – No.67). The necessary 'authority' (see No.74) exercised by the therapist sees to it that, whatever the current mood within the group might be, the session still retains, or regains, meaningful form (see **Gestalt** – No.25). Then any situation, no matter how turbulent, has gestalt, is purposeful, significant, a positive experience.

Example: It was the very wildest boy in the group who helped transform an absolutely chaotic situation into just such a significant experience. Somebody had put chestnuts into the drums and now they were flying everywhere chased by screaming children! The boy sang out:'Heute ist Kastanienfest!'

Heu - te ist Ka - sta - nien fest!

[*Today's our conker party!*]

An alert music therapist will appreciate the importance of such a response, which musically is a perfect, spontaneous expression of what has happened: 'Heute' (*today*, now) on the highest note and further emphasised by the dotted rhythm, the tension resolved by the falling fourth and the 'Ka-sta-nien' (*conkers*) ideally emphasized by the second interval in a regular crotchet rhythm. In a case like this the music therapist has to take the music very seriously!

Another boy, a seven-year-old whose reactions were violent and aggressive, summed up his reactions to an activity by singing the following at the end of the session:

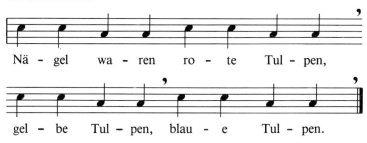

Nä - gel wa - ren ro - te Tul - pen,

gel - be Tul - pen, blau - e Tul - pen.

[*Nails they were like red tulips,
yellow tulips, blue tulips . . .*]

Another therapist had presented us with some large nails made up with crêpe paper to look like flowers. Her idea was that we would remove the coloured paper, hang the nails on our stands and play on them. This boy, however, had torn off the paper in fury, not in order to play on them but to use them as weapons. A dangerous situation!

His final contribution, sung spontaneously and without emotion, was like a confession in which he atoned for his wrongdoing.

20

Movement: *the* basic principle of life itself, all existence involves movement and therefore is subject to change. Nothing living is motionless, the changes may be more or less visible, more or less rapid. Growth is movement within the organism. So is decay. *All growth has to overcome opposition.*

Movement – Stimulation
Stimulation – Movement

Novalis

In Music Therapy:

Perception and movement are intimately related, the one determines the other. The new perspective that results from movement encourages perception, as long as this is at all active. With some forms of handicap it is not, or it can be so limited that it registers only a small segment of what ought to be discernible (see **Perception** – No.1). In therapy we encounter children who move about too little, or too much, whose movements are too exaggerated or too cramped. Well-thought-out activities can stimulate each child to different movements and this may, in time, help change his characteristic, spontaneous movements.

When movements are lethargic or the child shows no disposition to turn around or towards the therapist it may be simply that the stimulus is too weak (see **Perception** – No.1). In English as in German the word 'move' applies both to physical movement and inner movement (to be 'moved' by something). The prefix 'e' (ex) changes the Latin word 'movere', (to move) into 'exmoveo', 'emoveo', to agitate, to affect. And even the word 'motio' implies inner movement too, manifested in a show of emotion.

Just as physical movement stimulates inner commotion so can an emotional excitement lead to a physical reaction, or prohibit one (transfix). In his inexhaustible treasure trove of reflections, Novalis also speculates on this phenomenon. A child's natural momentum (the impulse gained through movement) can be seen in the way he plays on, say, a xylophone or a metallophone. A very young child's impulse will show short cycles of five or six strokes a time played in a pre-rhythmic and pre-melodic fashion. Regular or symmetrical movements (playing in time) will come later.

It may suggest a serious problem if a child always wants *only* to play in time quite undistracted by any emotion. By matching the child's tempo but introducing rhythmic variations,

or improvising a melody to his accompaniment, the therapist can make out of the child's playing something more interesting and turn it into an experience for him. The therapist will be pleased if the child breaks out of his monotonous playing and explores some other

22

possibilities (playing quavers for example). It is a paradox that playing strictly in time, so important in the training of a musician, is something the music therapist may have to 'untrain'!

21

Multisensory: simultaneously or alternately appealing to more than one of the senses. Strengthens the memory. Multisensory experiences create an awareness of parallels, develop the association of ideas.

In Music Therapy:

When children's interest in sound *alone* wanes, and experience tells us that purely acoustic stimuli will not always hold their undivided attention, then we can explore the optical or tactile aspects of our equipment. ('What's a cold instrument?', 'Which instrument is warmer?', 'On the xylophone, which is the longest and which is the shortest bar?')

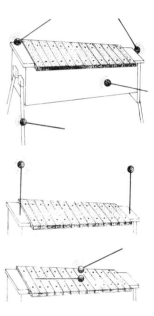

Example: A boy with Down's syndrome, who was already thirteen when he came to me, did not trust himself to play on a metallophone, for example. Of his own accord he did nothing, but a challenge could motivate him to lay some beaters on the instrument. I copied him and he seemed to enjoy the game. In the next session he was prepared to hold the beaters in his hands but not to play the instrument and I realized that further challenges would have no effect. He did, however, use the beaters on the wooden frame, the casing and the legs of the instrument, and would say that there were three legs, and so on. He played at setting up the beaters on the edge (flood-lights!) and letting them fall onto the playing surface (always making sure they made no sound when they fell), in (optical!) canon form too, one after the other. He went so far as to hit the head of *my* beater which I had left lying on the instrument and produced a sound in this way but was too inhibited to play directly. He was well aware that this could perhaps make demands on him emotionally. Always polite, his answer to everything was 'yes please' or 'yes, of course'. After our second session together I wondered if he had simply been trained to react in this restrained way. In the third session he managed to touch the metallophone just hard enough to produce a sound but he startled himself with this and, as had happened before, quickly wiped his beaters clean. The fourth to sixth sessions paved the way to a breakthrough and he was then able to play freely and confidently; the playing was pre-melodic in character but with a regular rhythm and even occasionally some individual rhythmic elaborations. *An optical and tactile exploration of the instrument had been necessary before he was ready to approach the acoustic side of playing.* I decided to record the twelfth session and was well rewarded! Sitting opposite each other we both played on an alto metallophone, an instrument he always preferred. When I asked who should start he said he would and he challenged me time and again to repeat what he had played, at first verbally ('now you') and later with quick gestures. Each phrase he played in one swift flourish and while I usually succeeded I was not always able to copy them exactly. My answer to very long phrases – of 25 notes or more – was a form of 'counterpoint'; my reply was deliberately shorter than his phrase.

This boy has already achieved a great deal:

1. he has overcome his shyness at playing at all
2. he can play a simple musical idea through to the end
3. he can play and ask his partner to respond (at school he will not speak at all)
4. he can steer a phrase, the style of playing and musical content, to a climax (see number fourteen in the following examples)

Only time will tell if he can progress beyond pre-melodic play or, indeed, if this would benefit him at all.

I have transcribed these (mostly pre-rhythmic/pre-melodic) phrases just as I recorded them in a twenty minute session. (Page 25)

The therapist repeats each phrase, sometimes in affirmation, sometimes as an echo. The examples up to and including number nine are selections while numbers ten to fourteen followed each other as shown.

I registered a metronome marking of approximately quaver = 196.

Some of our equipment emphasizes strongly the optical-tactile aspect. A colourful set of bars, for example (two pairs in yellow, three in blue, two green, two red, one orange), decorated with grooves and of varying lengths.

Such equipment can be set up in different ways, taken apart and newly formed, stimulating new associations of ideas.

A clever nine-year-old boy with autistic tendencies, always very isolated, would often build 'organ pipes' out of these coloured bars. He set these up in front of the metallophone on the side where the others could see them. He then played and said that he was playing the organ. A child new to the group asked one day where there was an organ and was disappointed when told, but to Sebastian it *was* one.

On top of one another they could form a house, placed lengthways a street – just two of the many possibilities that suggest themselves. When stood upright the large bars (approximately 20 cm long) are particularly unstable and fall over easily whether one wants them to or not.

Small children's natural urge to destroy their own constructions can be easily satisfied! We should not interpret this urge negatively. The child feels strong enough to build something new at any time and the rapid change between gestalt (see No.25) and chaos (see No.26) strengthens his self-assurance.

On the other hand, more complicated structures built by older children with considerable behavioural problems and a proneness to destructive behaviour are often carefully looked after and protected; the children say they must stay as they are forever. Constructions of this sort (adults would say they are quite impossible) require intuitive skill and patience to build (for example to construct a tower out of a variety of implements on a foundation of four large hoops and then to crawl inside without disturbing anything would be typical of such children!). In comparison adult patients would destroy an edifice like this. I remember one occasion when an empty xylophone had been stood on its side and decorated with triangles

♩ = c. 196

1. Up to the high G.

2. Up to the high A.

3. Mostly in the lower register and ending there.

4. In the middle register but ending in the lower.

5. Confidently into the upper register again, the comma preparing the way.

6. The phrase is developed further up to the highest notes.

7. Descending gently again.

8. Mainly descending.

25 |notes   30 notes

The phrases become longer and more intensive. As it becomes impossible to copy them exactly the therapist's answering phrases take on a contrasting character.

9. As a result the phrases become shorter again, more deliberate and melodic.

The examples 10 – 14 are played in direct succession – the therapist repeats each phrase exactly. Phrase 14 begins slowly, each note being played with an accent up to the climax on A. (Quaver = 160)

and cymbals and so on, but after dancing around it for a while it was sent crashing to the floor. I could sense, even while it was being built, that it was only a matter of time before this inevitable destructive climax occurred.

Building activities of this kind provide the patient with abundant possibilities to express himself and help the therapist in his diagnosis. On the other hand, accomplishing tasks in a working atmosphere of predetermined gestalt (simply recognizing the shape and size of a given object and placing it in the appropriate hole, for example) where the answer can only be right or wrong, represents a one-dimensional and not a multisensory activity.

Children in the stages before cognitive awareness begins to develop look upon 'music' as something that happens after a task has been completed. Three children of kindergarten age built a 'house' for their 'snakes'. The 'snakes' were two lengths of chain (see No.42) which are associated with snakes by most children. They were strings of shining pearls about two feet and three feet in length. The children built the house out of their stools and decorated it. Now that everything was finished, R. set up a glockenspiel in the house and played 'for the snakes'.

While we use our equipment primarily of course for its acoustic possibilities, it also serves for various multisensory activities which can:

1. heighten perceptive awareness
2. encourage associative thinking
3. compensate for a deficiency in one of the senses
4. develop more economical musical ideas

22

Association: a spontaneous mental connection, triggered off by a movement, a sound, a smell that recalls a previous experience. Opens a channel to that experience and recreates it uniting the present with the past. Comparable to a mental cord that suddenly and unexpectedly tautens, is activated. The word contains the Latin adjective 'socius' meaning 'taking part', 'connected with' and comes from the verb 'sequi', 'to follow', 'to accompany'.

To associate can mean one of two opposite poles: to generalize or to differentiate. A concrete aid to the memory.

In Music Therapy:

Association constitutes the very essence of our spirit.

Novalis

The ability to associate is an enrichment.

A tendency to make too many associations is distracting (one cannot see the wood for the trees) and must be reduced. Making too few leads to apathy, and stimulation is necessary. Autistic children with a high IQ and the ability to express themselves well rarely keep to a single activity or line of thought. Their mental manoeuvrability leads to unremitting associations in all directions and they can never experience what continuity means. This is a torment for them and irritates those around them. At school they are often rebuked and soon decide to say nothing at all until, finally, they are written off as apathetic and uncreative. As soon as they feel themselves understood or in a sympathetic environment, all that is dammed up inside them rushes out. In accordance with the ISO-Principle (see No.67) one must go along with the resulting flood of associations until it abates.

When the child's and the therapist's respective threads of associations run in quite different directions, the result is confusion and misunderstanding! The therapist asks himself: 'how on earth did he arrive *there*?' Yet another association!

23

Initiative: behaviour that begins something new, spontaneous self-expression, the opposite of imitative behaviour. At first, initiative must be accepted without criticism because disruptive initiative is a valid possibility. Does it really disrupt? As it introduces something new, initiative behaviour usually comes unexpectedly, and this has the same effect as disruption.

In Music Therapy:

Initiative behaviour is often found in behaviourally disturbed children with a higher than average IQ. They often 'catch on' more quickly than other children and they do not hold back their ideas or opinions but express them without a second thought. Not always easy for the therapist! He will need all his skill to accept and work with this, especially in group sessions. An 'experienced' therapist who has become too inflexible will find it most difficult to come to terms with such behaviour, with such surprises which each time require of him a readiness to reassess his approach. The group can deal best with spontaneous ideas. The foremost member is easily recognized and tolerated up to the point where he oversteps the mark with his initiative behaviour, becomes too disturbing, too irritating, and the group turns against him. Therapist and patients must discover the tolerance level of the group towards initiative behaviour (this can accept some excessive swings beyond its limits as long as the pendulum swings back and remains generally within its constraints).

Behaviourally disturbed children, and children with sense deficiencies, are generally the ones who bring the spark of initiative into the group. The decision whether to kindle or dampen this spark will depend on the situation and on the immediate therapeutic object-ive. Children who show symptoms of deprivation will not at first trust themselves to show any spontaneous initiative, but the correct therapy can in most cases bring about a breakthrough relatively quickly.

Mentally handicapped children (and the more severe the handicap the more true this is) show no real need to express themselves in this way. The therapist must ask himself, however, if a child is perhaps using his handicap as a cover, deliberately misleading those around him so that no demands are made on him. In the appropriate surroundings his behaviour will show surprising spontaneity, he will come up with new ideas more quickly than children one had considered more able and will trust himself to express them. If his interest is not awakened he will skilfully ward off all approaches, smiling his way amiably through the session (the therapist might easily find this touching), contributing merely stereotyped words and phrases, saying anything just to be left in peace. If a child with a low IQ shows much more initiative behaviour, and positive initiative, in therapy than he does elsewhere (at school, for example) then a reassessment of his IQ is certainly necessary. If this confirms the higher IQ that one had suspected then the therapist must work at breaking down the child's defences that prevent him always showing his true capabilities. It is important to distinguish between initiative behaviour (whether 'constructive' or 'destructive'), that shows abundant associative thinking, and the purposeless hyper-activity shown by the easily distracted child. He will stay only a short time with any one instrument or activity, contributing no personal ideas and showing no reactions to the work, either positive or negative. New challenges merely take him by surprise. To the onlooker he appears to be tormented by his inner restlessness. Initiative behaviour is encouraged in the OMT. It is welcomed because the child can show in this way what he is capable of, what he wants, what he needs (see **Over-challenging** and **Under-challenging** – Nos.18 and 19). It is by reacting to the child's initiative that the therapist can best help him (see **ISO-Principle, Unstructured activities** and **Association** – Nos.67, 41 and 22).

24

Tolerance: ability to endure something annoying, that annoys because it is different, or acts differently than one expected or would oneself. Tolerance assumes an understanding for 'otherness' and forbids an immediate reaction before one has tried to reach an understanding of the other. The capability to be tolerant can be acquired and consciously nurtured but is rarely innate.

In Music Therapy:

The therapist *must* have a tolerant nature! He cannot practise enough at acquiring and maintaining one. Tolerance stems ultimately from the belief that no child deliberately wants to be frustrating. A child's behaviour is naturally open and ingenuous (naive – 'nativus' = native). He 'acts' as he *is*. Untouched by other influences a child would never consciously offend. Childish behaviour is only offensive and deliberately disruptive if the child has been corrupted (by his environment) or is following an example. How much one should tolerate will depend on the particular case but tolerance does not mean acceptance of everything. The limit will be set, however, not by how much the therapist can bear but how much is still acceptable for the child before he damages himself further (see **Patience** – No.69). As far as this is possible, the therapist's reaction should be in accordance with the ISO-Principle (see No.67) and he will often decide he must be tolerant in opposition to his true feelings. Finally, the therapist should have no personal aspirations apart from being there to help. This requires having a whole wealth of resources at his finger-tips out of which he can call up the appropriate support at will. With each child he works with the therapist enlarges and enriches this store because each child is unique, and problems never the same. 'Normal' children can demand much more tolerance from an adult while children in need of therapy are likely to approach the therapist and his suggestions with an eager readiness to co-operate. The concept of 'tolerance' is to the therapist not simply a question of 'putting up with' something! (see **Patience** – No.69)

III Gestalt

25

Every form of life represents gestalt that lives out its peculiar development in space and time. Living creatures are, in a certain sense, structured time – like melodies.

A. Portmann

Gestalt: form that is both tangible and intelligible. An organized whole in which each part affects every other, the whole being more than the sum of its parts. End-product of actions or events. Possible in a spatial and a temporal sense.

In Music Therapy:

Gestalt should extend to the smallest constituent elements of an activity. In terms of music the simplest concept of form is playing – not playing, sound – silence, an apparently easy step that means a great deal to a disturbed or handicapped child.

sound	silence
me	you
me	us
temporal-spatial	
now	then
here	there
quantitative	
augmentation	diminution

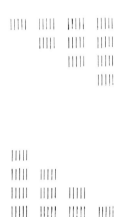

Examples of musical gestalt: One child begins to play, a second joins in, a third, a fourth . . . conclusion in a climax of sound – silence – a new beginning, this time with the second child. Alternatively, augmentation until all are playing . . . the first child stops, then the second, the third, the fourth, gradual diminution into silence – begin again. The playing here is basically pre-melodic in character but with a distinct rhythm and some small measure of melodic form in which the sound can be developed.

If we remove the middle bars (B flat, B) of a xylophone, for example, we are left with two distinct playing areas. We can play alternately on the one side or on the other; one child can play on the darker half, another on the brighter half.

One region is for the three roses standing in the garden while the other is for the fir-trees in the wood; the summer belongs to the roses, the winter to the firs. Musical gestalt achieved by means of a simple spatial re-arrangement.

Som-mer ist's lu-stig, im — Win-ter ist's kalt.

Sommer
[Summer] [Winter]
Winter

[In the garden three roses, in the wood three fir trees.
In summer it's cheerful, in winter it's cold.]

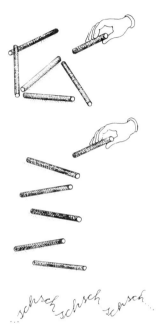

Example of spatial gestalt (visual): Sitting in a circle on the floor the children each have at least three claves. The first child lays a clave on the floor. Where to put his clave in relation to the first one requires a decision from the second child. Confronted by a developing form the third child's decision is more difficult, the fourth child's even more so, and so on. After three rounds a more or less recognizable or suggestive form has been created which can be discussed or applauded and is an incentive to a fresh start. More advanced children would create different, more open forms. Perhaps one child, impatient that his concept of how the form should develop is not shared by the child whose turn it is, cannot hold himself back and adds a clave out of turn; he should not be restrained – a measure of chaos is permissible!

Example of spatial gestalt (in movement): A ring of children walks to the centre of the circle chanting words such as 'huhu hulehuh', G.P. = short rest in intimate, dark togetherness, separation out into a circle again with words such as 'sisi sisisi' – da capo.

Or the 'seventh wave', the ocean's biggest. Wave movements, accompanied by sounds like 'sshhh sshhh', culminating in the seventh one which is the largest with the longest 'backwash'. Start again from the beginning.

It is in group work that gestalt is particularly necessary. Although this does not mean that the whole session must be dominated by an awareness of gestalt, its absence for longer periods of time will often result in the children losing interest. The young therapist tends to cling to his faith in gestalt and, because he believes in it so firmly, has most success with it. A therapist with the experience of countless sessions behind him is more wary of imposing form, trying instead to encourage gestalt to develop naturally out of the children's actions and reactions.

Gestalt in work with individual children is of a different sort. I can remember one seven-year-old boy who for several sessions did nothing but race around the drums in a large circle, screaming wildly, rejecting the confinements of anything more constructive. Only after he had satisfied this need did he speak, and then he made highly individual discriminations and comparisons. He attributed colours to vowels, was convinced that 'Ü' was bright green. He also associated melodies with moods and the 'gestalt' that he had created for himself stayed in his memory for a long time.

31

One of the most severely handicapped children in my experience was a boy who at the age of three had exclusively oral contact with objects. He bit everything that came within his reach and would never tire of this. The aim of his therapy was to break down this oral fixation and bring about 'hand-contact'. Within six months we succeeded in reducing by half the oral nature of his movements. The other half was now manual. He would take hold of and lift up a hoop, for example, and a remarkable fact was that he would lift the hoop to his mouth and let it fall again in a regular rhythm but without showing any tendency to bite into it. He progressed as far as to clap his hands together and tap other objects when the therapy unfortunately had to be broken off. The following gestalt had, however, also come about: he played on the big drum, typically for him, a fast rhythmic phrase (as always, only with his hands) and then paused. The therapist 'answered' him in the same way and then he played

again. Occasionally he sought deep eye-contact with the therapist. It happened only rarely but compensated by its depth and sincerity.

26

Chaos: the opposite pole to recognizable gestalt, but also its raw material. While it is not the therapist's aim to bring it about he should not be afraid of it. He should try to assimilate it as 'chaosgestalt' and mould it into something positive. Chaos as culmination.

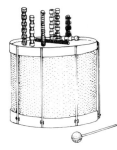

In Music Therapy:

A child is capable of experiencing chaos as a culminating point or climax; in this sense, chaos is gestalt without form – a paradox! (See the examples in **Multisensory** – No.21.) A building process culminates in destruction, in *fortissimo* so to speak. Coloured bars stood on end on a big drum might represent trees, a town or people: the child has built a pretty composition which an adult would probably want to add to or even, perhaps, develop further on an acoustic level. Not so a child up to about the age of seven. He will take great pleasure in destroying his creation and find this a satisfying climax, in *fortissimo*. He will immediately start to build again, working once more towards gestalt, perfectly confident that, 'I can do it again'. He needs and learns from this repetitive cycle. The child's awareness of time can be compared to a film running too fast. Catastrophes happen suddenly but the child can equally quickly switch over to the building-up phase and any intervention in this process by an adult might be an irreparable mistake. This is a fundamental problem for the therapist: which is more appropriate and when, structured or unstructured activities? The sensitive therapist with some experience will tend towards the latter. The presence of an attentive but non-interfering therapist is important for the child – feedback from him strengthens the child's self-confidence, provides reassurance and encouragement.

27

Order: concept of organizing objects or thoughts into a state of organic coherence. We distinguish between gestalt (an organized whole, each part affecting every other and all the parts working together towards a climax), and order (also 'orderliness') in which the parts are assigned places next to one another and each can be called up independently. *Order itself is essentially undynamic* but, while it is by no means a prerequisite, it can help to achieve gestalt.

Order for order's sake undermines man's essential ability to mould himself and the world around him.

Antoine de Saint-Exupéry

In Music Therapy:

Whether or not it is necessary to draw a particular child's attention to the question of order will depend on the nature of that child. Some children will come into the room and have no interest in doing or taking part in anything. The most they might want to do would be to tidy up and put away the equipment that has been set up for them, hoping that 'that's it' and they will be allowed to leave again! In less extreme cases, as soon as an activity is over a child may feel an urgent need to put the objects he has been working with straight back where they belong. An undynamic process! On the other hand there are some children for whom clearing away the equipment would be a beneficial therapeutic exercise.

The search for gestalt can often result in wonderful examples of 'decorated' order. Indeed, the Greek noun 'kosmos' means an ornament or decoration.

Examples of decoration: Each child in the group has a hoop on the floor in front of him which he decorates with anything he can find in the room that fits into his concept of how the hoop should look. This idea came from the children themselves and they were very enthusiastic! That the finished products should be preserved was explicitly demanded by some children and tacitly understood by others, a requirement that contradicts the needs of the children described in 'Chaos' (see No.26). However, the children in this example were already between six and seven years old. Or: the children decorate a tree stump whose many branches can produce various tones (a natural xylophone, so to speak) with unforeseen creative richness, showing a feeling for statics that few adults could demonstrate with such ease.

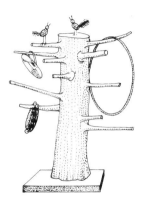

Children who seem to have no awareness of order are more effectively stimulated by an indirect approach (who can tell me where the drums belong? Where can we find the xylophones? *etc.*) than by being simply told what to do.

28

Ostinato: repetition of a fixed pattern in the realms of speech, physical movements or instrumental playing.

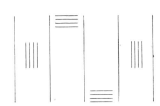

In Music Therapy:

An ostinato can be used as an exercise-ground to satisfy the child's impulse to repeat everything. With the mentally handicapped, and especially in cases of Down's syndrome, this can become a compulsive need. Together with a second, non-ostinato rhythm or movement, the ostinato becomes an accompaniment; a melody should eventually compel it to stop, to reach a conclusion. If this happens with mentally handicapped children it represents a breakthrough! With blind children too, who also often show a compulsion to repeat everything. In a social context, when two children play together, one the melody and the other an ostinato accompaniment to it, a bond is set up between them. Work with ostinati can even be introduced in cases of 'perseveration' (see No.30) with the therapist and child playing together (see the examples in **Practice** – No.31).

A *crescendo* (an increase in volume or intensity) or *decrescendo* (a decrease of the same) can lend gestalt to a simple ostinato pattern; accented notes can too. Stressing spatial ideas helps in the treatment of perseveration. A simple rhythm can be divided into right and left parts for a period of time by regularly accentuating certain elements with the words 'here' and 'there'; stereotype repetition can be avoided by a gradual *crescendo* throughout. With very little effort the repetitions in such an ostinato exercise can be made more interesting and significant: turning around while playing and pointing in a different direction after each repetition, for example. The ostinato as a component in composition work is effective with behaviourally disturbed children. I have observed how clever eight-year-olds were fascinated for a long time with a melody of only three notes that they had composed themselves (self-imposed restraint), repeating it time and again but always with an awareness of gestalt.

A pre-rhythmic, pre-melodic style of playing is a complete contrast to work with ostinati, but can be a stepping-stone to it. Any child who wants to work exclusively with strict ostinato rhythms should be encouraged to develop vital, pre-rhythmic impulses in his playing too. There are grounds for concern, for example, if a six-year-old boy, who wants to suggest thunder and lightning with his playing, tries to do so using only a regular rhythm because he lacks the confidence to play freely.

28a

Pattern: a small formula or motif in any one of a variety of different spheres that results in an ostinato if repeated continually.

29

Stereotype movements: manifest themselves in the form of constant and habitual physical movements, without purpose or recognizable significance, and give the impression of a 'still-life with movement'!

In Music Therapy:

Commonly found in children with autistic tendencies. Hopeful in so far as it is at least motion. The autistic child enjoys making such movements. To him they do have significance and indeed they may mean everything to him. Often revolving around a thread or some other scarcely visible object, the movements are always compact, circular ones while the body itself remains quite still. *The individuality of the child, his personality, is, in spite of the empty movements, still recognizably 'there'*. It is the easily recognizable and predictable nature of such movements that makes contact and therapeutic work at all possible. The therapist can copy the child's movements and in so doing make him conscious of them. *Stereotype movements give the child a sense of security*; he has a plaything always by him that cannot be easily taken away from him (and should not be). Stereotype words and phrases that only the child understands and whose meanings he guards carefully are a related phenomenon.

'. . . *amalgafei* . . . '

30

Perseveration: an extreme form of stereotype behaviour. The compulsive repetition of a pattern, or in most cases the endless repetition of a single action – a single, unvarying drumbeat for example.

In Music Therapy:

Perseveration is found in cases of severe mental disturbance. In comparison with stereotype behaviour one is much less aware of the personality behind the movements and we cannot point to any enjoyment for the child. From the very beginning of the treatment it is important to introduce some structural elements, even of the simplest kind: playing/not playing, playing in clearly different ways, alternating between 'I play/you play', or 'one child plays/everybody plays'. The child should find the structure attractive and transparent (the child sees what is expected of him). While autistic stereotyped behaviour should be accepted (played along with) the opposite is the case with perseveration. To do so would mean the therapist and patient together entering a blind alley from which there is no way out.

31

Practice: an activity lying between work and play. We gain practice at something simply by doing it repeatedly. The therapist's concern must therefore be to awaken and maintain the children's interest in an activity: as long as they are taking an active part they are practising.

In Music Therapy:
In therapy we distinguish between:
a) practice with an object or instrument
b) practice in social awareness
c) practice towards gestalt

a) practice is necessary in getting to know an instrument, what it can do and what one can do with it. The more the child plays an instrument, the better he understands it and the greater the interest in further practice/playing. A relationship with the instrument develops, *it becomes a partner*. Greater skill makes creative practising possible, new possibilities are discovered in the instrument, the child can express more of himself through the instrument; ever-greater potential as the relationship develops.

b) acceptance of others, 'getting on' with them, 'putting up' with them, requires practice. Tolerance of 'otherness', give and take. The ability to take a back seat, to allow others to act but to be ready with a contribution when required, carefully watching to see when that moment has arrived: all this must be practised.

c) practice at viewing one's own actions objectively, to be able to repeat, correct, develop and order them. This gestalt can be remembered, repeated, passed on to others or recorded.

At the pre-melodic stage the child does not practise (see No.35). He is happy just to play. He feels no need to play anything more than once and does not reflect on what he has played. A normally developing child goes through this stage between the ages of two and four; a handicapped child later. A severely handicapped child can never progress beyond it because he cannot, of his own accord, attain the condition that makes practice possible. A child's being able to reach this condition is therefore significant for his diagnosis and favourable for his prognosis. The child learns to control his (primitively) creative, mainly fortuitous playing, begins to think about what he has played and by repeatedly practising it, consciously shapes and amplifies it; it becomes a part of him. This is something quite different from stereotype behaviour where there is no possibility of development or variation, and no creative awareness on the child's part of what he has played. Practice strengthens the memory. Remembering what one has already achieved promotes the will to do it again.

Children need to explore instruments for themselves. For this reason the therapist should not instruct them in their use. That this confrontation with the instrument usually takes place loudly is natural. The Latin 'exploro' comes from 'ploro' which means 'loudly shouting', 'screaming'; 'exploro' itself means to explore an area. So noisy exploration is something quite natural! A 'this is how it should be done' approach to playing an instrument has no place in music therapy. (It is another matter when the child wants and asks for technical assistance.)

It has already been mentioned what an important step it is when a child becomes capable of practising (see **Memory** – No.12). Renée, who had been diagnosed as severely mentally handicapped, did just this. She had discovered a pattern and understood that it consisted of three notes played with a distinct rhythm (spatial awareness certainly led to the orginal discovery – the three notes were the last three on a xylophone). Over a period of more than six weeks Renée would play this pattern over and over again, starting as soon as she entered the room. One had to suspect that this was a stereotype movement. At the time she neither spoke nor understood speech. Her melody was made up of the three notes (f,g,a) at the right-hand end of the xylophone. As an experiment the xylophone was set up in front of her so that these notes were on her left. At first she played the last three notes on the right as usual but she noticed that something was wrong, that it sounded different, and she discovered and played her pattern again at the other end of the instrument. She found the solution by herself. Spatial considerations played no part, neither was her behaviour stereotype; she heard and recognized the melody. The therapist's attempts to develop this met with no success at the time – Renée ignored them all.

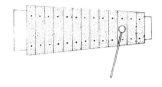

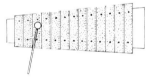

Later, however, she began to play her pattern again but always starting on the next note down, which gave the melody now a major, now a minor character.

In further sessions the melody was still made up of only three notes but an upbeat resulted in the following variations:

etc.

An ascending upbeat brought about a melody in 3/4 time.

In example 3, Renée combined the scope of her original melody (three notes) with a newly discovered four-note range.

Example 4 records what happened one day when the therapist spontaneously joined in with an ostinato quaver accompaniment. Rather than being disturbed by this Renée took up the challenge. Already after the first repetition she quickly signalled her intention to the therapist and then took over the lower part, changing back to the melodic upper part the next time round, without once interrupting the flow of the music. She now understood the meaning of playing together, of teamwork!

Renée's case history is comprehensively described in the OMT (pages 153–160). She came to music therapy at the age of three and a half when she could neither stand nor walk but only sit; she could not speak and had no understanding of speech. She could express herself only with a stereotype movement of her hands. The description of Renée in the OMT ends with: 'one will be able to expect more from her. The vocal expression will increase and before that she should be able to walk freely.' Both predictions turned out to be true. Now eleven years old, Renée can walk, understands speech and can express herself clearly in two to three word sentences. Without music therapy she would never have achieved so much.

Example of Marco: Absolutely nothing worked with Marco. As well as being mentally handicapped he was very restless and although he could speak he did so too quickly to be understood. He could bear to be in a room only for the shortest time before he sang out 'bye-bye, bye-bye' and wanted to leave. He could be persuaded to stay but obviously felt uncomfortable. A dramatic change took place when Marco discovered *his* instrument – the snare drum. He knew immediately how to play it. He had already become a 'virtuoso' on the xylophone, rattling off his hectic little phrases (playing slowly was a strain for him). At first his loud playing on the snare drum was difficult to bear. Eventually it became more bearable, less wild, and Marco could even play quietly if the occasion demanded. One well-known dance tune, the *Ennstaler Polka*, he liked to imagine played in F major 'for the boys' in a large dance hall and then in C major 'for the girls' in a small one.

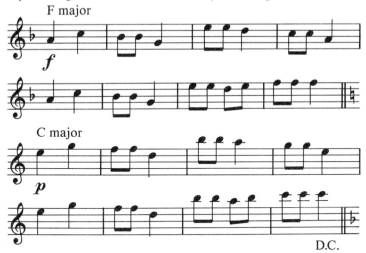

He was happy with this arrangement and could easily picture the two halls: in 'the girls' hall' he played a wonderful, if still very fast, *pianissimo* passage. At first he was rough with and scornful of his partner, a boy with Down's syndrome of the same age, but the more he achieved on his instrument the friendlier he became to Fabian. Whereas earlier he would take the big drum away from him to play it himself a little, he now took it *to* his partner and said, 'here you are Fabian, you'll need this.' If the proper beaters for the snare drum could not be found (other 'normal' children used them too, though nowhere near as skilfully as he did) then his search for them was tireless and he always found them eventually. He would accept no other beaters as a substitute and when he triumphantly discovered the right ones said to me, 'this time you must lock them away'. Since then I always do so!

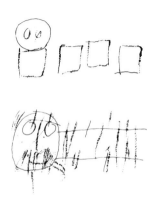

His own body was so underdeveloped that his drawings of people consisted only of the head drawn as a rectangle. He liked a song about a dragon however (a clearly structured activity for the group), which we played time and again, and his conception of the dragon became so concrete that one day he spontaneously went to the blackboard and drew it – head, body, facial expression and other detailed bodily features. Playing (practising) on his instrument had helped improve his outlook, his imagination and his performance.

32

Rhythm: an organized sequence of acoustic impulses with no particular musical pitch, whose structure is made comprehensible by a periodic succession of organic accents. The natural rhythms of any culture are peculiar to that culture and difficult for a stranger to understand or to copy. Even the apparently simple, regular 4/4 rhythms of our culture would be difficult for an African to reproduce, the rhythms of his culture equally difficult for us.

In Music Therapy:

A very small child cannot at first reproduce a regular rhythm. Exactly when an appreciation starts to be shown will depend on the child's development. With a normally developing child this will usually be in his second year. But even he will continue for a long time to express himself in a pre-rhythmic fashion when he is allowed to play an instrument freely and not obliged to play 'correctly' in time. Secondary imitation (see No.8) – a sort of unconscious long-term imitation – causes once-registered phenomena – words and phrases rhythmically spoken – to re-emerge from the memory, suddenly and unexpectedly, as if new: the learning process. A child will in this way progress naturally from a pre-rhythmic to a regular

rhythmic style if left alone and not obliged to do so too soon. On the other hand, once the child shows signs of moving out of the pre-rhythmic stage there should be no further encouragement to play in this way. (Pre-rhythmic musical ideas such as 'storm-music' or 'rain-music' should be replaced by pieces with a fixed rhythm.) If, however, the fixed rhythmic stage arrives or has been brought about unnaturally early, the deficiency in free rhythmic playing must be made up. *Music therapy does not consist solely of sounds and noises, the recognition of them*, and so on, important as this is (its importance is perhaps further increased by the need to offset the dominance of strictly defined musical forms today). Our work hovers around the dividing line between free and 'fixed' musical expression, both of which are important. It is up to the therapist to recognize at what stage of his development each child stands.

Making mud-pies is important, building complicated sand-castles equally so! After building a sand-castle there may return the need to make mud-pies. The therapist must take both seriously. He should not interrupt the organic flow of a particular rhythm and if it shows signs of progressing away from the pre-rhythmic style while the therapist is still working on this mud-pie stage, then the therapist must adapt; in other words, must act as a *therapist*. As teachers too we must oversee an organic development from free pre-rhythmic, pre-melodic playing to playing rhythmically and melodically predetermined 'pieces' of music. The child should not suddenly be required to learn to read music without any emotional impulse coming from him, nor should he be made to feel that free musical expression must no longer be taken seriously and music making can only be done with a music-stand in front of him; or that adults who do not play from music are not 'real' musicians. Music therapy exists today in this state of tension between 'pre-' and 'fixed'. Paradoxical-sounding comments such as, 'well after all, you studied music', addressed critically to the therapist, illustrate the political nature of this problem.

With mentally handicapped children it is very important to observe the natural way in which they express themselves rhythmically.

Example: The way two boys, both eight years old, both attending special schools, both mentally handicapped, expressed themselves freely in rhythm was totally different. When he was in a certain frame of mind one boy would set up his instrument against the wall (so that he could play for himself alone) and produce a steady, regular rhythm over a long period of time. It was possible, therefore, for him to be calm. Normally he was quite the opposite, restless and fidgety, and spoke too quickly to be understood. But this same boy was capable of performing the following game which he invented himself.

It began with an association of sounds. He had put the handles of his beaters through the holes in the wooden casing over a radiator by the window. As he turned them impatiently they continually struck the metal radiator underneath. The noise they made sounded for him (and subsequently for me too) like a vehicle travelling on rails. He associated it with a tram. (Coming to therapy meant a long tram ride for him and he was clearly acutely perceptive during the journey.)

He was now the tram driver with all the functions and responsibilities that that entails: driving, announcing the next station, stopping, supervising the passengers getting in and out, closing the doors, setting off again.

Firmly holding the 'steering-wheel' (the heads of two of the drum beaters that he had previously fiddled with so impatiently, one in each hand) he drove smoothly. He clearly and correctly announced each stop (about ten well-known points in the centre of Munich) and in the right order too:
'Ma-rienplatz' . . .
'Change here for the railway station' . . .
He waited patiently for the imaginary passengers to get in and out and then a forthright 'stand clear of the doors!' . . .
He shut the doors with a particular sound (this was my contribution to the game – I suggested it once and he never forgot it) and off he went again, bending down to another beater (the microphone) to announce into it quietly:
'Next stop Sendlingertorplatz' . . . slowing down, stop . . . Another wait for the passengers and then again an energetic 'stand clear!' (sometimes it was necessary to repeat this!). He closed the doors and drove off again, always moving the beaters gently to produce the travelling noise on the radiator. Again the intimate announcement into the microphone 'next stop Goethe-platz' and so on. At the stop he removed the microphone/beater in order to give instructions to the people waiting on the platform, importantly swinging the imaginary microphone-cord as he did so.

Later I was allowed to ride with him sitting behind him. I felt perfectly safe! – and wasn't required to get in and out at each stop!

After this game, which he performed with very little variation, he quietly took a bass xylophone over to the wall again and for a while calmly played a distinct (but pre-melodic) rhythm to himself; there were no elements of dialogue in what he played and no longer any imaginary audience.

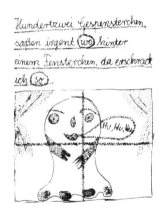

The second boy played (when he played at all) always with a *crescendo* and *accelerando* (a gradual intensification in volume and tempo) towards a climax; he then started again. He had to be especially motivated before he would start, proving the point that not all children have an interest in musical activities.

This child had been diagnosed as less able than he really was. He was always interrupting with new ideas and was a permanent disturbance; he soon landed in the lowest class at school which made his already disturbed behaviour even worse. In comparison with the first boy he seemed to have greater abilities but lacked any stability. Probably because he had not been correctly assessed, he felt a need to attract attention to himself and always be the focal point. Therapeutically the two boys must be approached in different ways. The first boy, who in his good phases could be calm, needed a stable, quiet atmosphere in which to develop his (limited) abilities as far as possible. The disturbing second boy, with his constant new ideas, needed to be given the possibility of carrying out some of them, with the therapist guiding them into channels that made them less irritating. It was important to treat his lively impulses with the respect they deserved.

Next to each other both boys would appear to be equally hyperactive and troublesome in everyday activities; the differences between them first became clear in their instrumental playing.

Children with hearing deficiencies who are otherwise normally developed soon start to play in regular rhythmic phrases, but these are rarely in 4/4 time. A pause before every repetition invariably results in a quasi 5/4 rhythm. In my experience a natural feeling for 4/4 time is exceptional and any attempts on the therapist's part to insist on this succeeds only in inhibiting the child's rhythmic self-expression. On the other hand I have often encountered distinct 3/4 rhythmic phrases. Even in verse, which we might expect to have an obvious 4/4 feel, the hearing-impaired child tends towards a free rhythmic form.

Example:

Hun-dert-zwei Ge-spen-ster-chen   *One-hundred-and-two little ghosts*
saß-en ir-gend-wo,   *sat somewhere*
hin-ter ei-nem Fen-ster-chen   *behind a little window*
da er-schrak ich so.   *and I was so afraid.*

The children brought this verse with them to the session; they had learnt it at school. As they recited it without the pauses that we would automatically insert, there was at first no recognizable rhythm. When the therapist drew their attention to the way it would be more effective, they were keen to try this out. The therapist made the inevitable minims on the words 'wo' and 'so' even longer and emphasised them with movements: 'wo' (*where?*) by looking around with a questioning look, and 'so' with a look of horror. After an initial protest the children caught on and liked to copy this exaggerated performance. It had, however, no lasting effect on them and they soon reverted to their natural 'irregularity'. I can still remember N's rhythm:

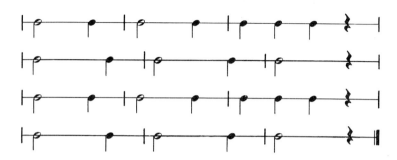

33

Pre-rhythmic: usually coupled with pre-melodic playing – a free rhythmic flow with no fixed structure or regular pulse (barring). Typical instrumental style of the small child.

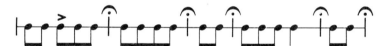

In Music Therapy:

A pre-rhythmic style of playing drums, triangles, *etc.*, but also of melodic bar instruments does have some small elements of form; typical are the pauses and new beginnings in the above example. *Pre-rhythmic playing movements are not stereotype movements.* It is very important to determine which kind of playing a child is demonstrating. Before a child expresses himself in our customary rhythmic forms he plays in a pre-rhythmic style. The first recognizable rhythms are probably a result of secondary imitation (see No.8),

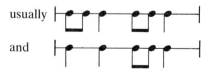

There can, however, also be a direct link with the child's motor development.

34

Melody: an arrangement of single notes joined together in succession; we distinguish between melodies with and without an upbeat. In our culture the melody will tend to be in regular bars of constant length and four to eight in number. The intervals between the individual notes, their musical relationship to each other, will determine the quality of the melody. The more personal experience is expressed in a melody, the better it will be. Any arrangement of intervals that is based on other, mechanical considerations alone (optical or numerical ones, for example) will, however perfect the construction, lack the qualities of a living melody that clearly has its origins in genuine personal experience. Carl Orff said, 'a good melody is like a smooth pebble', a comparison that also emphasizes the important elements of time and resistance. After thousands of years in the water a stone becomes smooth and almost 'malleable', it feels 'soft' to the touch. The quality of the stone (its hardness) seems to find expression in its very opposite. This image could equally well apply to the genesis of a vital, lasting melody.

In Music Therapy:

A child can experience a melody without feeling the need or having the ability to play or sing it. In my experience, the ability to pick out the notes of a melody on an instrument (a piano or the melodic bar instruments, where all the notes are readily available, and not on the guitar or violin, for example) is possible, depending on the child's ability, from the age of five, and is normal at seven or eight. A song or a melody can transport a child into another world: the world of role-playing.

This was the case with Dan.

He was just five and liked coming to music therapy. He had a remarkably deep voice as a result of necessary hormone treatment during long and frequent hospitalization. His whole personality together with his deep voice seemed to make him a grown-up partner. Musically, he liked to express himself on the percussion and was proud of himself one day when I wrote a rhythm of his on the blackboard (I wanted to remember it).

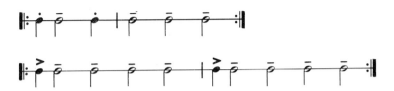

(and later)

In the third session I played and sang him the following song:

Hop hop hop zu Pfer - de, wir rei - ten um die
Er - de, Er - de, die Son - ne rei - tet
hin – ter-drein, wie wird sie a - bends mü - de sein.

Night-time noises

[*Let's ride off on horseback
around the world and then right back,
the sun is riding right behind,
at night he will be tired you'll find.*]

'That was pretty, will you do it again?' I did so and he came, with a little white horse he had found among a collection of articles on the window-sill and took part. The horse rode along the edge of the xylophone in time with the music. Dan stood up and fetched a little tiny bird as well. When I repeated the song a second time he let the bird fly over the horse which now hovered over the surface of the xylophone. Suddenly he became really involved . . .

To add some variety to the song I had added a 'night-time' sequel – night music, tranquillity, daybreak, invitation to the bird to fly with us. During this sequel he suddenly startled me, 'Shhh . . . there's an evil spirit', in that deep voice of his! The next 'morning' I called on the bird, 'the sun's risen, the horse has been saddled, will you fly with us?' 'No, the evil spirit's been and the bird's ill!' He wanted me to play the whole song again though. Night-time came around again – again the menacing hiss from Dan and, in the morning, again, 'no, the evil spirit's been and the bird's ill!' Six times in succession the same story! The seventh night passed quietly without any interruption and in the morning my challenge to the bird, which had previously been in vain, 'the sun's risen, the horse has been saddled, will you fly with us?' was received with: 'yes, today it's possible, the evil spirit hasn't been'. He stood up saying, 'now let's play some music', went over to the percussion instruments and uninhibitedly played some strong, happy and very individual rhythms. The song, together with an intensive instrumental accompaniment, had not been 'music' to him.

Pre-melodic: 'musical' expression which results in no recognizable melody (in the accepted sense) and cannot be repeated. A very young (two-year-old) child's typical style when he has the opportunity to play on one of the bar instruments (glockenspiel, xylophone, *etc.*). *Physical impulses working on a melodic playing surface produce a pre-melodic style.* The melodic flow is periodically interrupted by pauses, each section containing, according to my observations, anything from five to twelve notes; in some special cases the 'phrases' may be longer (see the examples in **Multisensory** – No.21). Elements of individual self-expression *are* contained in such musical efforts which can, therefore, be taken into account when assessing a child's capabilities. (This style of playing is not, as is often implied, just a matter of aimlessly hitting the instrument.)

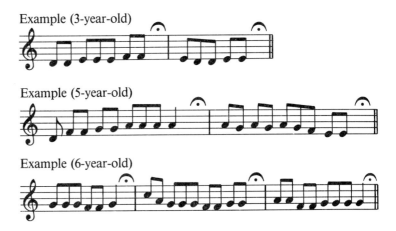

Example (3-year-old)

Example (5-year-old)

Example (6-year-old)

In Music Therapy:

Left alone, a normal child likes to express himself in a pre-melodic way up to about the age of seven. He will give free rein to his physical impulses which, from about the age of four, can be clearly structured rhythmically. Such playing will develop naturally into the typical melodic style of our culture. When behaviourally disturbed seven-year-olds create a melody, they will usually restrict themselves to three or four notes. Children with learning difficulties will stay longer in the pre-melodic stage to avoid greater demands being made on them. For children with Down's syndrome, with the exception of especially talented ones, genuine melodic playing is too taxing.

Pre-melodic playing gives hearing-impaired children the possibility of uninhibited self-expression, of creating pictures in sound that 'say' something to them simply by means of their own natural, unrestrained physical movements; motion as a form of auditory experience.

The pre-melodic stage is necessary and a child will stay in this phase until he is *ready* to produce a thought-out succession of notes that he wants to repeat and retain. An appreciation of economy in the choice of notes will come naturally, either because the child feels 'safer' with just a few notes or because a small group of notes is optically easier to locate on an instrument. The child decides for himself what notes to work with – another criterion for assessment.

Example: Randy, a seven-year-old boy who had enormous difficulties at school both with his fellow pupils and especially with his teachers, and whose writing was also very bad, based his first melody on optical considerations – he chose the three highest notes on the instrument.

He repeated his melody-pattern several times before retreating behind his stool taking paper and coloured crayons with him and furtively setting to work. It took several minutes before he triumphantly showed me the letters of his three notes, written in large, ornamental capitals.

The next time he expanded his melody; now there were two parts.

Again he retired to draw. Again he re-emerged with his three capital letters but drawn differently this time. Usually, when required to write, he was reluctant but here he found enough motivation to do so of his own accord!

36

Interval: possible in time or space, from the Latin 'intervallum' meaning 'the space between ramparts'. Musically an interval is the difference in pitch between two sounds situated next to each other or further apart. Pre-melodic playing takes no account of intervals; the child jumps from one note to another as if on the same plane. A conscious use of intervals includes an awareness of the intervening space, the 'jump', between the notes together with a sense of 'high' and 'low'. This is a three-dimensional awareness that includes the harmonic possibilities of the two notes (a rampart, too, includes a lower part that goes into the earth and gives stability, and an upper part that is visible). The 'three-dimensional' aspect of any interval can be emphasized by harmonizing it with the 'missing' notes (see **Harmony** – No.37). The intervals themselves, the varying amounts of space between the notes (a second, third, fourth, fifth, sixth, seventh or octave), each has its own particular dynamism.

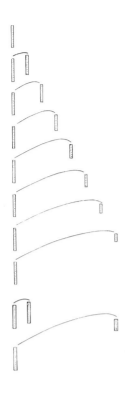

In Music Therapy:

On our bar instruments, with their limited and easily comprehensible playing areas (in contrast to that of a piano, for example), work with intervals can at first be visual: discovering the smallest and the largest intervals possible. An acoustic awareness of the space between notes will develop gradually. This conscious ordering of acoustic phenomena means that the days of 'innocence' in musical expression are over. As therapists we must make sure that a child's desire to 'get it right' does not mean a complete disregard for spontaneous self-expression. One cannot stress too strongly the importance of free, pre-melodic expression. Its powerful expressive potential can make a melody appeal strongly to the emotions. For this very reason a child may instinctively avoid it under certain circumstances.

Examples: I was touched one day (it was the last session before Christmas) when an emotionally disturbed twelve-year-old boy, who suffered very much from having no friends, asked me in a roundabout way, and barely audibly, to play *Silent Night*. He learnt it during the session and played it on all conceivable bar instruments, three different xylophones, two different metallophones and glockenspiels. At each new instrument he said, 'it works on this one too!' (the boy was of only average ability). In the first session after Christmas he tried to play it again but, when he did not manage it straight away, threw away the beaters in fury.

One neglected five-year-old boy, (he had no father and his mother was an addict) whose IQ was judged to be only bordering on the normal, recently surprised me with some letters that he wrote on the blackboard. He had asked me what he should write. I said he should make a house. He asked 'a real one?' and I nodded. He did not, however, *draw* a house but wrote HOUSE almost perfectly in capital letters. Then he spotted my typewriter and insisted on writing with it. I saw that he was determined to write his name, Daniel, without any help and he managed it. We wrote it in red and black, small and large letters. I pointed out that on the instrument that he had previously played so well in a pre-melodic way he could play 'D' and 'A' (a fifth) as in DAniel. He came over, saw what I was doing and said, 'You play that, I'll write some more'.

Although the interval of a second itself is aesthetically appealing, when a child feels an inner compulsion to use it in every session, and then repeatedly, it suggests a condition of anxiety that must be treated therapeutically.

If a child of ten still 'plays around' in a pre-melodic way the therapist should suspect that he is deliberately avoiding the responsibilities involved in (self-)conscious musical expression.

37

Harmony: the third component in the structure of music, after rhythm and melody.

The Greek word 'harmonia' means literally a joining together – a binding together of parts into a concordant or agreeable whole, of individual steps into flowing, uninterrupted movement. It referred also to the tuning of an instrument – into which mode – the Dorian, Phrygian, Lydian, *etc*. The different effects that these various modes had on the inner feelings both of performers and listeners was understood by ancient Chinese cultures and put to socio-political use.

In Music Therapy:

This structural element of music has no 'pre-' stage corresponding to the pre-rhythmic and pre-melodic stages. Many children can play together in a pre-melodic way without adjusting to each other or having to play 'correctly'; mutual tolerance is all that is needed to make this 'harmonious'. Once the step has been taken to an awareness of music (of a 'piece' of music) as consisting of various 'parts', then playing together in harmony is more complicated and the 'innocence' of the previous phase must be left behind.

Playing with an appreciation of musical harmony becomes relevant from about the age of eight – with gifted children often earlier. Mentally handicapped children usually fall behind here. While they may sense the harmonic elements of a melody when the therapist plays it to them, and while the harmony certainly shapes and stabilizes their feelings and reactions, they can rarely accomplish the art of playing in harmony themselves. Behaviourally disturbed children of the appropriate age can understand harmonic progressions and carry them out but they often prefer not to make the effort.

Most folk songs and folk dances in our culture are based firmly on a tonic-dominant principle, that is they consist of an organic movement back and forth between two chords, one based on the key of the melody, the tonic, and the other based on the fifth note of that key, the dominant.

This regular to and fro lends stability to a melody: we wait for the expected alternation which *will* come. Two opposites are reconciled – they complement each other. One refuge is left but only for the safety of another and this gives a feeling of security. The organized division into two and the compelling alternation in the construction of these songs and dances produces an organic movement within their structure: the tonic can be understood as a reinforcement of one's own 'standpoint', the dominant as a movement towards a different one before a return to one's own. There is no danger of getting lost. Tonic and dominant are an evocation in sound of the duality that is a part of our existence: day – night, man – woman, sun

– moon, growth – decay. Such considerations underline the fundamental significance of harmonized music. The subdominant (the chord on the fourth note of a key) is the third important step. It introduces a new emotional aspect too. It surprises and also broadens the scope of the melody, adding a new dimension so to speak – the 'up' on top of the 'right-left' division of the tonic-dominant interplay.

As therapists we must be well-versed in the rules of harmony and have them at our finger-tips for whenever children show a need for them (see **ISO-Principle** – No.67). It is extremely unsatisfactory if a therapist is so unsure of himself that he has to steer the session in another direction at such times.

Examples of some children's understanding of harmony:

Karin, a blind girl, had been adopted at the age of one-and-a-half. With love and patience the new parents succeeded in making progress with their very reserved child so that damage caused by her deprivation was gradually made up. At three she came to music therapy, into a small group of blind children. Here too she was very reserved, only very gradually taking in what was happening and needing time before she would feel her way to an instrument or another child. Then, however, she overtook all the others in terms of interest and ability. At six she was able, after listening to and practising it a few times, to reproduce correctly a melody by Bartók. She simply *wanted* to so much! With her left hand she felt her way around the bars of a xylophone or metallophone and played with a beater in her right hand, so gaining an understanding of the spaces between the notes of the intervals.

At seven she was ready to accompany a melody. We set up a bar instrument in front of her so that one area contained the three notes of the tonic and another those of the dominant. In this way she could, although blind, easily find and play the harmonies that she could already 'hear' in her head. She played with great enthusiasm, correcting immediately any mistakes she made. Whenever she played anything through without a mistake she cheered loudly, 'goal!' The explanation: it had been explained to her that this cry at a football match meant that something had been done well. She naturally used it now herself!

Another blind child, Paul, reacted quite differently. He could recognize melodies and even gave them names, but he rarely played them. If we played a song, a Bavarian *Ländler* for example, (i.e. something that simply *demands* a strident tonic-dominant harmony) with an accompaniment only of fifths, he thought that this sounded good. If we built deliberate mistakes into our accompaniment he thought this sounded even better! Finally, when two therapists accompanied the song with a completely random selection of notes he said: 'It gets better and better all the time!'

IV Object

38

Object: past participle of Latin 'obicere' = to 'throw', literally something thrown up in opposition, set up against; something one is confronted with, that one must come to terms with.

In Music Therapy:

It is the instruments we use that bring objectivity into the relationship between therapist and patient. These 'objects' are principally acoustic in nature, ones that resound well. Movement impulses (stroking, hitting, plucking) make them sound. Strictly speaking, completely non-acoustic objects do not exist but the resonance of different objects varies in quality and degree. At first a child will be interested in what *every* object sounds like when struck. At the same time the child is exploring his motor energy (see **Practice** – No.31), and the effects of his efforts (the sounds he produces) provide him with a tangible guide to the relative strength and dexterity of his motor development. A child in need of therapy will usually exaggerate, playing too loudly or too softly depending on his nature. He finds a 'normal' style of playing uninteresting. Behaviourally disturbed children are often accused of being too noisy or too quiet. Their approach to an instrument and the way in which they strike it give clues as to their impulses, their frame of mind and the state of their feelings. The child has to discover the correct amount of 'resistance' to the instrument that he feels is required, so *any* contact with a resonant object brings experience and understanding of his at first ungoverned, later tamed energies. Observing this process of discovery provides the adult with a wealth of material for therapeutic work. The child must be given the freedom to play as he wants to – ISO (see No.67). This gives the therapist the opportunity to decide on a future course of action.

'How did the sound get into the stone?' asked Thomas.

Only by overcoming resistance will you make something of yourself.

Antoine de Saint-Exupéry

Example: One thirteen-year-old girl, at home domineering, but in strange surroundings very shy, played mainly in seconds on the xylophone or metallophone. Doing this meant that her hands were nearly touching and her shoulders hunched (see **Anxiety** – No.46). The 'cramped' sounds she produced were a reflection of her state of mind. Our aim at first was to encourage her to spread her arms in order to relax her shoulders. Simply telling a child to do this is certainly pointless if not actually harmful. Imaginative movement exercises can help. For example: playing two hanging cymbals placed a short distance away to the left and right of the child. Or: running in a wide circle around a kettle drum and at the same time playing it with one hand. To make sure the circle stays wide one could place

51

a cymbal just within reach but outside the circle that has to be played each time round as well. Verse can help too, for example: 'Hat Füße und geht nicht, hat Federn und fliegt nicht' (*What has legs but cannot walk, what has feathers but cannot fly?*).

The solution to the riddle (a bed, an eiderdown) is not important here. Reciting it rhythmically, the part about the feet calls for heavy stamping while the part with the feathers is an invitation to 'fly' around with outstretched arms. The girl cited above gradually improved; she spoke too, even loudly.

Our objects, the instruments, are used for (spontaneous or controlled) playing in structured or unstructured activities (see OMT).

39

Rules: 'rules of play' can introduce or increase suspense but can also inhibit it. Under certain circumstances rules can result in the state of suspense between a child and a person, activity or object being disrupted.

In Music Therapy:

Easily understood rules can produce an atmosphere of heightened suspense: 'let's do it *now*', 'let's do it *right*', and consequently 'you're doing it *wrong*'. Mutual observation (to see if the rules are being followed) encourages critical social awareness.

With the behaviourally disturbed, where unstructured activities are usually indicated (see No.41), rules that are seen to be fair can often work wonders. Rules that the children set for themselves are often the most effective and they are adhered to much more strictly than many adults would to their own rules. *Rules can mean stability and security to a child; something 'to hold on to'*. With mentally handicapped children, who often show little initiative of their own, rules can compensate and set things in motion. An initial, simple rule can be made more complex by a second, even more so by a third and so on: this is linear co-ordination as described in the OMT (p.53).

Examples of simple rules in instrumental playing: (with a group of about six children). Each child has a bar instrument. The inevitability that all the children would play in the same sort of way and at the same time led to the following rules of play. Whenever X, who has no instrument, steps into the circle everybody plays but as soon as he leaves the circle everybody stops: X completes the 'sound-circuit'. A sound complex arises that allows each child to play as he wants to. Result: sound-silence. The rule can also be turned around, as it often will be when working with the behaviourally disturbed.

Another example: a child can only play after his instrument has been 'ignited' with a blow from his neighbour. He then plays for as long as he likes after which he strikes his neighbour's instrument, passing the turn on, and stops. This rule produces a situation that has two facets. Firstly, a child *enjoys* hitting his neighbour's instrument – whether aggressively or not – which is an incentive for him not to play too long. Secondly, each child has the opportunity to play alone with the others listening attentively waiting for the 'hand-over'. An effective rule! The therapist must accept the fact that rules have a limited life-span. In the last example the rules of play are broken when a child wants to 'ignite' two neighbours' instruments at the same time. The game may continue for a while but the rules are no longer being obeyed. There is no need to restart the game and insist on the old rules. Something is probably happening within the group that is necessary and should be allowed to develop (for further examples see **Structure** – No.40).

40

Structure: from the Latin 'structura', an orderly construction, a superstructure.

In Music Therapy:

Careful thought and planning can lead to well-structured sessions. The session is most likely to go according to plan if the planning is done with the particular children who will be attending the session in mind, their possible reactions and so on. While structure is necessary (and the therapist should always have some reserve plans up his sleeve) nothing could be more wrong than to want to keep to the plan at all costs. It can be interesting to try out the same plan with different groups and observe how each group transforms the plan and makes it its own. As a general rule, structured sessions are necessary in the treatment of the mentally handicapped (see the schema and explanations in **Unstructured activities** – No.41). *Structure provides stability*; it can be gradually extended and relaxed.

Structure without life is dead.
But life without structure unseen.

John Cage

Structure can be achieved by means of:

1. a song
2. a rhythm
3. imitation
4. a rule

1. A song provides structure
a) 'A little girl drives the geese out' – tableau
   There are two characters, the little girl and the bush. The girl is the one who goes away, sees something, speaks to it and goes home again. The bush stands by the path, is met, is spoken to and stays where it is (page 55).
b) 'In my father's garden' – tableau
   About a person who falls asleep and dreams that snow is falling on him (illustrate musically). When he wakes up he sees that it was the roses

above him (also describe in music). In the third stanza there is a dance (possibilities for *tutti* playing and acting); he wants to go home with his love but sees that the house has disappeared.

In the last stanza they build a house (page 57). (This song was very productive when performed with a group of severely spastic children, one of whom was also blind. The less the children are able to do by themselves, the more must be happening in an activity: singing, suitable accompaniment, snow falling, *etc*. Each child will be able to take part in at least one of these activities. Building the house might perhaps motivate a spastic child to raise his arms to make the roof or a window that he can look through.)

2. Rhythm provides structure
a) A child invents a rhythm-pattern on chime bars or a drum and the group tries to play it too. The rhythm could also be developed on a visual level: playing high above the head or down on the floor, and so on.
b) Pass an object around the circle in time with a particular rhythm.
c) Make a given rhythm more complex by subdivisions or omissions; turn it into a game, playing the rhythm on various instruments and moving in time with it.
d) Other possibilities of all kinds will depend on the strengths and capabilities of the children.

3. Imitation provides structure
Many possibilities using both sound and movement. One should not insist on exact imitation; it is enough if the spirit of the original model is reproduced.

4. A rule provides structure (see the examples under **Spontaneity** – No.44)
Generally speaking children love rules, especially if they can make them themselves.
a) Keep moving as long as we can still hear a large cymbal and then stop. Everybody will usually stop at once.
b) Think of a spot in the room that one will go to. After a signal to start everybody walks to his spot. No common ending results. A very individual activity, often almost meditative in character.
c) See **Rules** – No.39 for other examples.

What should the therapist do when confronted with 'pointless' rules that a child insists he follow? For example, 'Look what I've got, do you see it? Now close your eyes and tell me what I'm playing!' The boy had shown me a triangle that he played after I had shut my eyes. Now I was supposed to guess what it was! My answer was, 'you played the triangle very nicely', and he was delighted, 'yes, look, look!' I had reacted correctly in the spirit of the 'activity-cycle' that should not be interrupted. According to Craig (1918) such an 'activity-cycle' is made up of three phases: an anticipatory, an appetitive and a consumative phase. It can be harmful to a child if the last, consumative, phase is cut off. Under certain circumstances he may suppress any further thoughts about the activity; dissatisfaction or anxiety may set in. Or the child revenges himself by

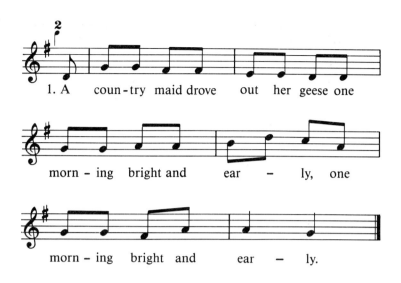

1. A coun-try maid drove out her geese one morn-ing bright and ear - ly, one morn - ing bright and ear - ly.

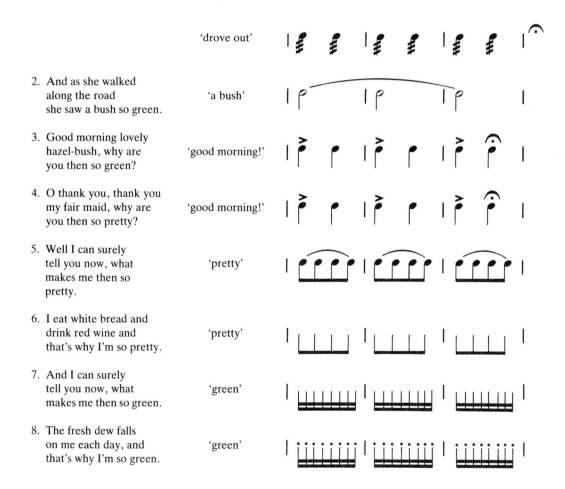

'drove out'

2. And as she walked
along the road
she saw a bush so green.

'a bush'

3. Good morning lovely
hazel-bush, why are
you then so green?

'good morning!'

4. O thank you, thank you
my fair maid, why are
you then so pretty?

'good morning!'

5. Well I can surely
tell you now, what
makes me then so
pretty.

'pretty'

6. I eat white bread and
drink red wine and
that's why I'm so pretty.

'pretty'

7. And I can surely
tell you now, what
makes me then so green.

'green'

8. The fresh dew falls
on me each day, and
that's why I'm so green.

'green'

aggressively unleashing what is dammed up inside him: he plays the clown, for example, floundering in a flood of monologues that he himself cannot stem and that eventually leaves him drained and miserable.

It is difficult for the therapist to find anything positive in meaningless rules but if he really takes the trouble he may. For example, some rules may demonstrate a quite different time-consciousness . . . 'somebody else goes into the middle as soon as the marble has run all the way through (through a 'Kugelturm' – see the illustration) with 30 cups.' The rule sounds reasonable enough, but we were seven in the group and, as the child well knew, a marble needed roughly 45 seconds to complete the journey! And *seven* rounds! The game lasted two rounds before an impatient boy said, 'that's enough, let's run all the marbles at the same time!' Reflecting on the 'slowness' of the boy who had suggested the rule I realized how inadequate my treatment of him had been up to this point.

41

Unstructured activities: the therapist brings no particular, predetermined plan to the session. The activities that result usually develop a structure of their own.

In Music Therapy:

Unstructured activities are appropriate in therapy with individual children but also with some groups, especially with the behaviourally disturbed.

Strictly speaking, no session is completely without structure:

– the room,
– the length of the session (usually an hour, but never less than thirty minutes),
– the objects – the children will expect to find the same equipment again,
– the members of the group,
– the mood and 'character' of the group.

All these factors are essentially elements providing structure.

'Unstructured activities' does not mean that the therapist takes no part in the proceedings. Ideally an attentive, impartial presence combined with a readiness to step in and help when necessary should be our goal: 'when should I intervene? Now perhaps? Where is all this leading? Why is he or she not taking part?' . . . Such considerations will occupy the therapist until he decides his assistance is required. The desire to help together with a professional eye

One sum-mer in the _ gar-den, I lay me down to

sleep. I dreamt that snow was fal - ling, was

fal-ling o-ver me. _____ I dreamt that snow was

fal - ling, was fal-ling o-ver me.

Music and movement: 'falling snow'

2. I woke up from my dream
   and saw the 'snow' was red!
   it was the bright, red roses
   that swayed above my head.   'red roses'

3. I wove a pretty crown,
   of all that I could see,
   I gave it to my love
   and bade her dance with me.   'dance'

4. And as the dance was at its best,
   the music ceased to play,
   we wanted to go home but
   we had no place to stay.   'no home'

5. I built for us a house
   of parsley fresh and green,
   with lilies and red roses,
   the finest ever seen.   'building a house'

to see when he should intervene are 'all' the therapist needs! The following schema demonstrate the relationship between structured and unstructured activities:

structured ||||

unstructured   ≡

The first symbol suggests a 'training-area' where the result of the various activities is cumulative. The second symbol suggests a dynamic 'force-field' of individual activities.

Only rarely will these schema be found in 'pure' form; corresponding, on the one hand, to initiative coming exclusively from the therapist, and on the other, to the therapist leaving all initiative to the dynamic impulses of the children. In practice a mixture of the static and the dynamic will be necessary.

With deprived children and the not too severely mentally handicapped the symbol might be drawn in this way: the therapist's suggestions provide a firm structure while dynamic initiative from the children is present in the ratio of 1:3 ⧢

An even balance between impulses from the children and intervention from the therapist might be relevant to children with sense-handicaps; ratio 2:2 ⧣

The ratio 3:1 – predominantly impulses from the children, timely intervention from the therapist providing stability – can be recommended with the behaviourally disturbed. ⧥

The symbol will rarely be seen in the ratio 4:0 except in the form of ⁞⁞⁞⁞ The explanation: a child shows no further interest and shuts himself off to everything the therapist can offer. Small gaps in his defences provide the only possibility for therapeutic intervention but this soon comes up against the next barrier. In his important book *The Empty Fortress* Bruno Bettelheim gives a detailed account of autistic behaviour. In my experience, defences, once breached by the therapist, are not restored again. The child has 'accepted' the therapist's intervention and does not relapse into a state of resistance or indifference.

42

Chain: a connected series of links usually of the same material used to secure and bind. Can also be joined to itself to form a ring. The concepts in the present book hang together like the links in a chain, one joined to the next, conducting the spirit of an idea through the book. As in a chain of pearls, between larger pearls is a succession of smaller ones; but each link in the chain is important. Significant too – while other fastenings may be rigid, an essential characteristic of a chain is its flexibility.

In Music Therapy:

Our use of chains is primarily tactile and optical rather than acoustic. One day, more or less by chance, I brought a chain of pearls to a session. It became known as the 'silver' chain and was followed later by a 'golden' one. The children love them and use them in a variety of different ways. What fascinates them above all is their brilliance and their flexibility (they seem to have a life of their own). A chain can often be a first point of contact (with autistic children). For children who can speak it is almost always a 'snake'. It encourages role-playing. Even a child who is difficult to motivate and shows little initiative will pick up a chain and let it drop into a large glass bell-jar where we keep it; the bell-jar rings as he does so. Dropped onto a drum, both the chain and the drum produce a sound. Blind children are also excited by them. The chains are not joined up but open like pieces of string and, as they are of different lengths (one two feet long, the other three), they are often used in competition with each other. Two five-year-olds made a 'house' out of their stools for the 'snakes' (see **Multisensory** – No.21) and decorated it with bells and other little objects. When the work was done they spontaneously began playing for the snakes (or for themselves?). Music as summation, climax, fulfilment.

A therapist's spontaneous reaction during a game as one boy suddenly played out of turn, 'you're breaking the chain', clearly affected the boy deeply. Two weeks later he used the same expression with me: apparently I had corrected him in some way and he said, 'but I didn't break the chain!'

43

Play: put simply, the opposite to work, obligation, purpose, exertion. Play takes place within a framework of time and space, and sometimes in one of numbers and topics. One plays *with* somebody else, which can also mean *against* them. Music can also be played alone where one's only 'partner' is the instrument and what one has expressed *through* the instrument. Genuine play relaxes although in a 'charged' atmosphere; tension is an intrinsic aspect of play. A contest is no longer play.

We play only with that which plays with us too.

All our playthings are playmates; we in turn are their playthings.

F.J. Buytendijk

In Music Therapy:

In music therapy we 'play with music' – rules are not necessarily taken into account. *The elements of music, sound and movement, can be enough.* The music we make is inspired by our surroundings and by our state of mind, our moods and our feelings. If we are not inspired by these then we cannot make music. The music therapist soon learns that children are often not in the mood for music: lack of emotion, fear of emotion, fear of beginning something new, fear of doing something wrong are all possible reasons. A surfeit of music

The necessary frame of mind for play is by nature unstable. At any moment 'normality' can re-assert itself, assisted either by an external event . . . or by an inner change – disillusionment or disenchantment paralysing the mood for play.

J. Huizinga, in Homo ludens

'consumption' might also be the case. This highlights the importance of the multisensory possibilities of our equipment. Sound itself might play no part in our work for several sessions although in the long run we should not allow another means of expression (painting, building, *etc.*) to be dominant. Our 'playing area' is the instrument; our movements, conditioned by our motor impulses and our motivation, provide our playing with a time-framework. Intensive self-expression (see **Cantus** – No.76) is our objective. Intense involvement with the music (see **Elevation** – No.6), if only for a few bars, is to be hoped for. Such intensity is healing. Observing the way a child plays can help us to a diagnosis of his state of mind.

The effects of music, of sounds can be surprising: a reserved child may become bright and cheerful, an unruly, over-spontaneous one calm and serene. Playing assumes a *vis-à-vis* even if this is only the instrument itself. Playing cannot therefore be an egocentric activity. We inevitably encounter and have to come to terms with 'somebody' – if only with a mirror image of ourselves.

Imitation, an important part of the therapy, must also be playful.

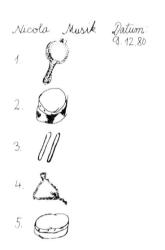

Nicola, a girl of ten with a hearing loss of 110 decibels (therefore effectively 'deaf') thought up the following game. She had collected various percussion instruments, which we often used, and stored them behind her stool. She gave her partner Julia, a girl with a similar serious hearing deficiency, exactly the same materials.

Now Nicola hid behind her stool and played an instrument. Without looking, Julia, sitting ten feet away behind *her* stool, was supposed to play the same instrument! Nicola also made a sketch of her instrument and challenged Julia to do the same. Later they compared their drawings. The whole affair was arranged in the shortest time (this quick understanding and agreement is typical of children) and carried out equally rapidly. 'Music', the name and the date were added afterwards and I was presented with the document.

Play must be distinguished from perseveration and stereotyped actions. Play has a beginning and an end. At the same time it is a state of things, a condition that 'lengthens' and 'fills' time. *A protective hand is also necessary*; play can result in the intense state of 'elevation', a delicate condition that can easily collapse.

Andreas Flitner describes some of the basic elements of children's playing (his observations are based on B. Sutton-Smith's *The Folk-Games of Children*, Austin, London, 1972):

a) an enquiring element
b) a building element (with blocks or sand)
c) an experimental element (with technique and dexterity)
d) an imitative element (acting, role-playing)

60

If we examine music in the light of these four categories:

a) Enquiry:
   The sounds, the materials (wood, skin) and the mechanism of the instruments can all be investigated. With this knowledge a child can relate to the instruments.
b) Building, organizing:
   Individual sounds played together build sound-complexes. Building is possible in a literal sense too. Constructions can be made out of the objects and then decorated (see **Order** – No.27).
c) Practice:
   Playing is at the same time practice – how does this sound, how quickly can I play, how hard do I have to hit this instrument, which beaters sound better, how loudly can I play, how quietly?
d) Imitation, role-playing:
   Sound is rarely an objective experience for a child but is associated with an idea, mood or situation. The therapist must be careful not to confuse this with his own associations!

As we can see, the possibilities presented by our acoustic and non-acoustic instruments (objects) correspond exactly with the general observations about the way children play. These elementary music objects should also be employed in the same way as other playthings, that is they should have no particular function *per se*. On no account should the child's free imaginative expression be hindered in any way.

Examples: To a four-year-old girl – suffering from fits of a psychological nature that eventually cleared up completely – triangles, little cymbals or bell-sprays hanging on their stand meant things to be sold. They were carrots or milk or whatever. Remarkably, one carrot might be a triangle while a second one was a cymbal. The child could be helped considerably by a period of completely unstructured activities. Little by little the therapist introduced his suggestions or instructions – the child should become accustomed to accepting other people's ideas – in carefully calculated doses. Her one session each week had a positive effect on her. Her mother told me that for three or four days after each session she was relaxed and unproblematic.

To a twelve-year-old girl with minimal cerebral palsy and some cognitive deficiencies, the beaters were people. She knew exactly which beater was the doctor, which the mother, which the baby, which the nurse. Whenever I was required to take part she corrected me immediately if I thought the blue beater was the mother instead of the doctor, for example. She would not tolerate any deviation from her appointed system.

Wulf showed me what a serious business play can be. He was an extremely behaviourally disturbed boy of six, and verbally very aggressive. He was in care and the consent of his natural mother was still needed for his adoption. He was of average ability, had little interest in music and was emotionally unstable. But he liked to paint! Then he could become really involved. And how did he paint? . . . He took a soft, white drumstick, dipped it in a piece of coloured material (we have many such pieces of material in various colours) and 'painted' an imaginary picture on a drum. Suddenly he screamed, 'S**t! There's no water'. I was about to say that he knew exactly where the water was, when he picked up a coloured bowl and said, 'ah, here's some water, now it's O.K.' He mixed together 'paint' and 'water' and painted the wall – 'careful, it might splash!' – with straight, vertical lines.

Or: with a group of eight-year-old boys, a beater became (at the suggestion of the therapist) a candle that had to be blown out to end a game – in one breath was the original idea. Not so Rasso: he blew and blew but the candle would not go out. He raced around the room with his burning candle to the screams of all the other children, shouting 'it's still burning, quick a fire-extinguisher, help, help!' until he succeeded at last in putting it out.

44

Spontaneity: the concept of an action occuring with no other motivation than an individual's impulse (external causes or conscious volition play no part). Inevitably the action might occur at the 'right' moment, but is equally likely to occur at an unfortunate moment or at quite the 'wrong' moment. Therefore, spontaneity is not always convenient!

In Music Therapy:

Depending on the situation, spontaneity is something to be encouraged, released or checked. Behaviourally disturbed children with a high IQ often find it difficult to hold back their (usually good) ideas. This makes them disruptive at school and, when their ideas are not given the attention they deserve, their reactions are violent. In the therapy we should give their ideas due recognition but at the same time try to arrest the flow. We should make it clear to them that we appreciate how quick they are, see that they are right or know that they have understood but that a period in 'neutral gear' would be a good idea. It will help if we make this waiting period interesting. For example: play a rhythm leaving out various beats, or playing only the rests. Such an exercise with a group has a socially binding effect as eye-contact is necessary if everybody is to play the same rhythm correctly. Similarly with a piece of verse: each member of the group recites it silently to himself with just certain words spoken out loud: 'Morgen, morgen, nur nicht HEUTE, sagen alle faulen LEUTE' (*tomorrow, tomorrow, but not today, that's what lazy people say*)

Heu - te,   Leu - te.

or the children might walk around the room in time with the rhythm occasionally chanting the words when they come up. Any variations in the game that develop may be interesting. The children might crouch on the floor ready to jump up as soon as a noise is heard. Or they may have to keep a set number of hoops spinning constantly until the end, the whole group being responsible for the success of the game.

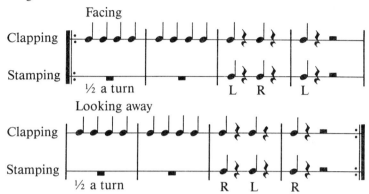

Possibilities with the instruments: each child invents a signal that becomes his own 'signature tune' with which he can be called up by the others.

Children will usually invent extremely characteristic signals.

a) spatially discovered, resolving chords

b) a little tune

c) lots of notes running up and down

d) one note repeated quickly

The idea of 'ignition' has already been described (see **Object** – No.38). A game of this sort is a good opportunity for observing how a child plays: does he copy the child who played before, does he clearly do the opposite, or does he act quite independently of the others?

A mentally handicapped child usually shows too little spontaneity and needs encouragement. Or his spontaneity can be somewhat absurd. Fabian, a shy, timid and inactive boy, would occasionally trust himself to tell stories but they were strange ones about ghosts and nasty giants and the like. He became loud and bossy and frightened the other children. My first reaction was to steer him towards another activity but then I let him complete his story two or three times. At the end (when an end came!) everybody applauded and he was satisfied. This was the same boy who suggested the impossibly long rule described in No.40.

A child's spontaneity can also be his downfall! The 'blind' girl described in No.16 could see the bird – and said so. A fourteen-year-old girl, Alma, did not speak at all but suddenly surprised us with some rhythmically well-pronounced reactions – 'aha', 'so-so'.

a - ha   so - so

Refreshing and welcome surprises. The way in which Alma usually automatically offered to shake hands while sporting a friendly smile was really a safety mechanism. It enabled her to evade any demands made on her. Undeniably a 'comfortable' existence but one which precludes the possibility of any progress.

45

Decision: a situation that confronts us when an intellectual boundary has been reached: this way – that way; yes – no; alone – together. Usually a choice between two directions.

In Music Therapy:

Structural components – such as space, time, subject matter or the group – lead to this situation. A child may demand decisions (of the therapist or himself): where should I play, when, on which instrument and with whom? Making a decision is as difficult for over-active children who want to do too much as for inactive children who want to do nothing. A decision represents a step towards overcoming a complex; it can also result in greater self-control. If we regard decisions as a higher grade of impulse we can see how they should not be over-encouraged too early; to a certain extent decision-making can inhibit a child's impulses. A child may require that the therapist make a decision or he may demand it of himself. All considerations of form inevitably mean that a decision must be made.

In spite of, or even because of, the possible inhibiting effect mentioned above, decisions should play *some* part in the therapy from the very beginning – playfully provocative: 'should I or will you?', 'loud or soft?', 'now or later?' Straight away boundaries are set and an awareness of them instilled in the child, even in cases of severe mental handicap. Even, for example, children with Down's syndrome who so like to remain with a single activity – so much so that perseveration can result. If variety is present from the beginning a child finds nothing unusual in it and even grows to expect it.

However, as with all therapeutic work, there can be no general rule. A badly timed encouragement to progress to a contrasting activity may abruptly disturb a child who is just beginning to be fascinated by his present one. Here, too, the 'dose', the 'how' and the 'when' are of decisive importance.

46

Anxiety: a distressing condition of insecurity that can take away one's breath or even temporarily paralyse. Danger, or a situation that one can no longer control, can bring it about but it can also become a permanent condition as a result of an occurrence that is re-lived time and again. An anxious person's fear may seem to have no readily apparent cause. A complete lack of anxiety is dangerous however – there is no sense of danger and no consciousness of situations that may get out of control.

In Music Therapy:

The music therapist is confronted with both 'fearful' and 'fearless' children; predominantly the former. Virtually every child experiences anxiety before the first therapy session. The therapist must counteract this immediately, but how? Verbal reassurances or a friendly look are not the answer. Without any ostentatious self-effacement the therapist should withdraw to a position of benevolent presence and allow the room and the objects in it free play. His contribution might be seemingly accidental, rudimentary challenges: lightly playing a drum, making a cymbal sound and other encouraging gestures designed to win over the child.

And the 'fearless' children who storm into the room and take possession? The therapist can best tackle such children with a healthy sense of authority, the strength of his personality and, above all, by making the child aware that his needs are of sole importance. An initial phase of observing the child, of taking in his personality, gives the therapist an understanding that then makes therapeutic intervention possible.

Examples: Two cases spring to mind of children coming to terms with their anxiety. Both centred around a kettle-drum that the children played on. One six-year-old boy's playing was pure motor energy – wild with no further attempt to express himself. At the time I would have had to conclude that he was not very talented or intelligent. However, after he had put this phase behind him, he surprised me with the range and sensitivity of his associations, a quite remarkable memory and extremely original ideas. His development proceeded normally and he no longer needed therapy.

The other boy, a seven-year-old, spoke about his anxiety. Running around the room he associated with 'deeper and deeper into the wood'. Breathless, he cried 'I'm not afraid yet' until he came across the witch and then he would always be roasted alive. One day, however, he said 'today the witch has made something special'. I asked what it was and he replied 'scrambled eggs and mashed potatoes'. The witch was being friendly. His usual *fortissimo* playing on the kettle-drum was toned down to a more normal level. He then sat down with a guitar and improvised ballads describing strange and frightening things. A simple accompaniment in one position underlined what he was singing.

Experience tells us that children's behaviour often contradicts the true state of their feelings. An anxious child, perhaps even paralysed with fear, may be longing to do something but simply does not trust himself to. A loud child who apparently has no fear at all, may well be putting on a show to mask his anxiety. He does not trust himself to be inactive, quiet and reserved. The therapist, his perceptive powers at their most acute and working in accordance with the ISO-Principle together, perhaps, with the occasional unexpected move, will succeed in discovering the child's real state of mind. The secret of therapeutic work lies in the 'dose'.

47

Trust: unlike anxiety, can hardly be present at the beginning of the therapy but is a condition that develops as child and therapist work together.

In Music Therapy:

The therapist's main concern must be to establish a relationship with a child based on trust, and to do this without any unnatural familiarity, over-friendliness or demanding too little of the child (see **Under-challenging** – No.19). The first sign of trust is friendly eye-contact. Important too is the state of the room, the atmosphere, the whole ambience. The objects in the room are there for the child; for him to play on, to be played to him. Unspoken but understood, 'you are here, we are glad that you're here, this session is for you'. Trust grows out of the feeling of security instilled in the child and is nurtured on the knowledge that he can expect to find the same atmosphere in all subsequent sessions. The memory of the previous session that the child takes away with him is not disappointed by the reality of the next session (see **Cantus-memoria-meditatio** – No.76).

Every aspect of a music therapy session – the room, the objects, the sounds, the activities, the possibilities and even the therapist himself – contribute to the development of trust in the child. He takes this trust away with him. Of course, as with everything that we 'possess', there is the danger that it might be lost or taken away. But until that time, if it should occur, such an 'inner' acquisition and enrichment is one that is most likely to be durable. We, as music therapists, should be able to give a child this priceless commodity. Something retained in the memory means something learnt. The trust that a child takes away with him in his memory after a therapy session is at the same time the fundamental and indispensable basis of learning itself.

48

Distance: possible in space and time. Similar to the concept 'Interval' (No.36), but whereas interval refers generally to various uniform degrees of intervening space, distance (also remoteness) describes the relationship between people and objects.

In Music Therapy:

Observing the distance between a child and an object, or instrument, (does he distance himself too much, or too little?) helps the therapist form a diagnosis of the child. An instrument represents an objective factor in the personal relationships formed during the therapy – between child and therapist or child and child. *It is at one and the same time a means of communication and a 'barrier', bringing individuals together but also establishing the necessary distance between them.* The more a child becomes involved with an instrument and identifies himself with it, the more he (temporarily) distances himself from his neighbour whilst at the same time developing another means of communicating with him. The instrument takes on the function of refining the relationship between the two, away from the level of direct, everyday communication. Clearly, therefore, it is extremely important that an anti-social child, whose behaviour is too direct and violent, should develop a relationship with an instrument. The quiet, reserved and over-cautious child needs time before he can approach an instrument. But once he has trusted himself to overcome the distance between himself and the object, he will often tend to prefer this means of communication to direct speech. *Eye-contact has the power to bridge distance.*

V Space – Time

49

The ramifications of every individual personality extend beyond the historical perspective into the realms of the metaphysical.

Erich Neumann

Space: is defined by its limits. A clearing in the middle of a forest gives us a sense of space. It is within the space created by the confines of a room or a house that we live and feel.

In Music Therapy:

The space, the room, in which therapy takes place should be attractive, orderly and stimulating – and uncluttered. It is the room that a child remembers; he looks forward expectantly to seeing it again. It brings an element of structure into the most unstructured activities.

A space is filled by an activity; also, the activity takes place within a certain space – of time. All that has taken place in a room, all the activities it has experienced, enrich its significance. It should remain a constant factor in the therapy.

50

Limits: a spatial concept – divide here from there, inside from outside, the known from the unknown, the near from the distant. Some limits can be broken, some should be, others may not be. Order, singularity, structure (whether in time or space) – none of these concepts is possible without limits. The body itself is a limitation.

In Music Therapy:

In our work we are constantly confronted with limits and limitations; they are often the reason why children come for therapy: limited development or limitations in their visual, acoustic, sensory or social capabilities. These limits must be expanded or, as in cases of uncontrolled behaviour, they must be re-established. The instruments themselves have their limits. A drum-skin is surrounded by a rim, the bars of a xylophone are contained within a wooden casing; the cymbal, though, vibrates in its entirety, to its own limits.

An unmanageable child, out of control, finds possibilities in the instruments for self-limitation; he expresses himself on the limited playing surfaces which 'respond' to his ideas – they resound, which is itself a temptation to stay within the limitations of the instrument.

On the other hand, to the deprived child, apathetic and withdrawn, an instrument is a bold venture, giving him the chance (if he dare take it) to step outside of himself, away from any stereotype movements and beyond the confines of his own body. An optic angle of perception of only 60 degrees can be considerably expanded to the right or left, up or down, by a resounding cymbal; sound leads to a greater awareness of space as one looks for it, reaches out for it. *A phenomenon of sound: it can stimulate action.*

51

Time: is always present but permanently changing. One of the secrets of life. Measurable but ultimately immeasurable.

In Music Therapy:

The length of a therapy session *is* measurable. It should be determined in advance: between 30 and 60 minutes, seldom less. Apart from rare exceptions, this predetermined length of time should not be exceeded. Knowing that time is limited is in itself a valuable stimulus. Time *during* therapy, however, cannot be measured chronologically. As in play, time can be experienced as 'short' or 'long' irrespective of what a clock says. Time spent at such activity (time that has been shaped and formed) has later and lasting effects and also helps train the memory (see **Cantus-memoria-meditatio** – No.76). When the therapist plans the time to be spent in a coming therapeutic encounter, he will also dwell on the time spent in previous sessions. His considerations then influence what actually happens; they cannot determine it. Planning for the time to be spent together can only mean reflecting and cautiously feeling one's way towards future time. This is especially the case when one is expecting very active children full of initiative.

52

Time-consciousness: individual perception of the length of a given period of time.

In Music Therapy:

The children should find the time spent in music therapy pleasant with an interesting mixture of activities – slow, fast, calm, lively. Our allowing (encouraging) initiative behaviour means that a session may run quite contrary to our expectations. The present mood of the group must be seen almost as a structural element of the session and treated accordingly. Generally speaking, a calm, uneventful session is not what we are looking for.

A melody almost always 'stretches' one's time-consciousness. If we play or sing a musical theme and then unexpectedly ask somebody how long they think it had lasted they will without exception judge it to have been much longer than it really was. Considering that such a melody lasts only a matter of seconds, it would be extremely difficult to fill an hour-long session with melodic material alone.

Examples of the duration of various nursery rhymes:

Three blind mice	= 16 sec.
Baa, baa black sheep	= 16 sec.
Humpty Dumpty	= 12 sec.
Jack and Jill	= 12 sec.
Polly put the kettle on	= 8 sec.
Nuts in May	= 12 sec.

Sixteen seconds is roughly the time it takes to breathe in and out four times. The melodies timed were all played at a normal tempo.

Themes from classical music present a similar picture. Mozart's Piano Sonata in C major K545, for example. The theme of the first movement (the first four bars), played calmly as it should be, lasts 8 seconds, and forms the basis for a whole sonata! The theme of *Eine kleine Nachtmusik* (4 bars) is played in only 6 seconds! These 8 or 6 seconds are all that are necessary to begin such works. In my opinion 'filled' time seems to last much longer than 'empty' time. When I am busy, time does not seem to 'fly' (many people are of the opposite opinion).

Whether a melody is played simply or with embellishments also influences our time-consciousness. We make the same mistake here for which children often earn a wry smile from us when *they* do it: as Piaget pointed out, an object appears bigger when divided into parts than when left whole. There seems to be less chocolate in a whole bar than in the same bar divided into, say, eight pieces!

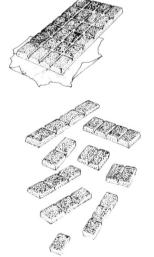

Calmly (approx. 8 sec.)

6
Fast (approx. 8 sec.)

Our time-consciousness can be accelerated by some instruments and slowed down by others. Instruments that require only a little effort to make them sound and whose sounds linger in the air (metallophones, cymbals, gongs) can have a calming effect, if one is already so disposed. Instruments that produce short-lived sounds (for resonance they require more strokes, and more skill) can have the opposite effect. The muffled crashing noise made by a Kugelturm (see **Structure** – No.40, p.56) filled with marbles will, if the feelings are given free rein, calm an over-excited person but enliven an over-passive one. The sound seems to make the patient aware of his state of mind and stimulates a change. We can observe this process happening without having to intervene in any way (see **ISO-Principle** – No.67).

53

Growth: increase in size over a period of time. Derived from the Indo-Germanic word 'vaksh'; the unseen essence of the growth process cannot be missed in the final, onomatopoeic 'ksh'! Growth and decay – the fundamental antithesis of life. The fact that growth is a laborious struggle is conveyed by the initial consonants of the Latin 'cresco'. The symbol for growth and decay is the moon, 'semper crescens et decrescens'.

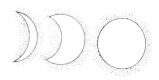
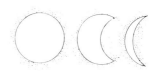

In Music Therapy:

As the process of growth works from the inside outwards, from the hidden to the visible (from a nucleus within a seed to a tree, within an egg to a fully fledged bird), it is not always measurable. Growth requires external nourishment which is assimilated into that which has already developed, becoming a new part of it. The quality of the nourishment is therefore important. Growth is the most essential characteristic of childhood. The 'normal' child needs little encouragement to accept nourishment (in all senses of the word); an adult determines the quality of that nourishment. The handicapped child has difficulties in accepting and assimilating nourishment. He lags behind. Therapy is often a matter of making up for interruptions in the growth-process. We often hear that a child's speech appeared to develop quite normally until about the age of two when his receptiveness was suddenly sealed off. Receptiveness is more

It takes one ten years to develop a good idea.

Camus

than a passive process of receiving; it also involves the active process of assimilation. Why such a 'refusal' to grow or develop further occurs (for example, in speech development) is not clear. Our task is to begin again at the point where the child blocked off further growth; where the assimilation of language stopped and the existing vocabulary began to diminish. The controlled use of phonetics and of pre-rhythmic and pre-melodic impulses may help. Physical and mental development go hand in hand; a five-year-old may look like a two-year-old. To return to my previous onomatopoeic illustration: the child's development has stopped at 'va' without reaching the mystery of 'ksh'. We must help the child to recover this loss.

54

Newness: usually thought of as a desirable condition. New opportunities, leaving old, perhaps unsolved problems behind. We associate newness with innocence and purity.

In Music Therapy:

Reactions to newness are often extreme: some children demand it exclusively while others reject it completely. At the one extreme, fear of the new: who's there, where is it, what should I do? At the other, unconcern and indifference: here is no different from anywhere else, I'm not impressed, I'll do what I always do! Fear of responsibility towards something new, or almost complete lack of such responsibility. Newness should have a cleansing, relieving effect on the children, allowing them to discard the old, the used, the no longer necessary. They can abandon themselves to a new situation. This should be relatively orderly and attractive, full of objects that stimulate the children, making them want to handle them, use them or try them out with each other.

55

Emptiness: void of content and therefore usually used in a negative sense: vacuity, nothingness. But the concept of 'emptying oneself' is a common religious and philosophical practice: emptiness has the potential power to absorb phenomena.

In Music Therapy:

Being able to 'empty oneself' is an ability that the therapist must develop: receptive, open – also open-minded, wanting nothing for himself, having no other wish than to be there for the children. A child can easily trust himself to cross the threshold into this emptiness. In an empty room there are no obstacles for him to stumble over; he can move around freely, placing objects himself when or where he pleases.

An empty room represents a salutary challenge to an aggressive child. Emptiness has an affinity with the immaterial and the spiritual, and makes corresponding demands on the child. Everything that he brings into this emptiness comes from his own creative imagination.

In one sense a comparison is possible between the antitheses key/ lock and emptiness/fullness. If the key stands for the therapist whose task it is to 'unlock' the child and unleash all his potential abilities, so the child now represents fullness, the content (negative content is also possible). All the side-effects of a handicap – aggressiveness, negative feelings, stress – can be unburdened into the receptive emptiness of the therapist. What is the active agent in the therapy? Is it the music, the objects or the therapist? Ultimately it is the therapist if he is able to offer the child this receptive emptiness. A deeper analysis of the emptiness reveals in its inner recesses a source of energy that, when necessary, will be stimulated into action. What the therapist absorbs provokes a reaction in the form of a powerful and instantaneous impulse. The immediate re-establishment of the condition of emptiness that follows such a reflex 'interference' is what makes the reaction therapeutic. The better developed this reservoir 'emptiness' is, and it is possible for the therapist to work at and improve his capabilities, the more effectively 'therapeutic' his therapy will be (even if this is not always immediately obvious).

56

Economy: deliberate giving or withholding of a commodity that one has or acquires. Intelligent administration, regulated dosage.

In Music Therapy:

Carefully considered 'dosage' is an important factor in the therapy. Material should not be wasted. Our maxim is to make a little go a long way. The result is a rich concentration of material both in the multisensory possibilities open to us and in the possible interchange of gestalt from one sphere to another: acoustic gestalt expressed in gestures, rhythmic gestalt in movement, a verse takes on melodic form, and so on. A simple rhythm is transformed by syllabic emphasis; a different vowel, or a mixture of vowels would introduce different colours and new dimensions.

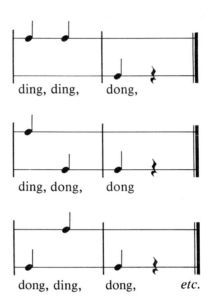

ding, ding,   dong,

ding, dong,   dong

dong, ding,   dong,   *etc.*

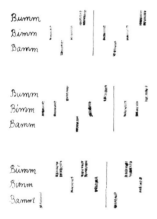

Gestures can also play a part, a gesture indicating a particular vowel, for example. Two drums might be found that correspond in pitch to two vowels used to illustrate different pitches. The rhythm could be 'harmonized' by the simultaneous use of various vowels. A xylophone would add a melodic dimension. Children able to comprehend it will appreciate this demonstration of the manifold possibilities inherent in a minimum of raw material. The designated relative pitches of the various vowels are often experienced quite differently by children with hearing deficiencies, as the example here shows. When asked where the different vowels were 'situated', Berndt's answer was 'the Bamm' is nearer than the 'Bimm' and the 'Bumm' is a long way away!

A gifted child has imagination and finds this intensive use of few ingredients easy to understand. The same applies to most behaviourally disturbed children who are normally gifted. Mentally handicapped children on the other hand need to be encouraged. This encouragement begins with the most elementary form of gestalt: action-inaction = playing – not playing, movement – rest, *etc.* and develops later into 'you play a note' – 'now I'll play one', 'first a note here – now a note there', *etc.* Out of some initial subject matter that is itself usually simple, concise and economical, the therapist can elicit an abundance of content. *Economy is the indispensable precursor to gestalt.*

57

Fullness: an end-product of appropriation and assimilation. Fullness implies full; too much flows over and *should* overflow. Living 'to the full' means taking from this abundance and replacing it with new content. Awareness of and respect for this fullness gives confidence.

In Music Therapy:

Only limitation or restriction can give us a true awareness of fullness. If a little is already a lot then how much more do all our objects represent that we can offer the children. Badly managed fullness cannot be comprehended and leads to chaos.

During a sesion with behaviourally disturbed and slightly mentally handicapped six-year-olds the idea arose, as each was sitting on the floor in a hoop, that they should decorate their hoops, should *fill* them. Each child combed the room for objects that he thought most suitable: large objects such as drums and gongs, but small ones too – bell-sprays, tops, model horses and birds, *etc*. There were no arguments but each child simply headed resolutely for whatever objects were still available. The result: four wonderfully individual 'garden landscapes' that we then made music with, first one after the other and then the whole ensemble in harmony. The children's final word was that we should leave everything exactly as it was.

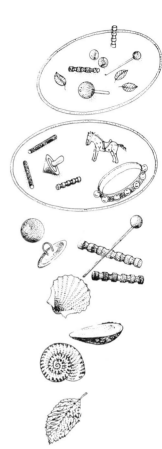

58

Surroundings: sometimes we can determine them but we must usually accept the given conditions.

In Music Therapy:

The surroundings are a constant factor even in unstructured therapeutic activities. Only in rare cases can we select the room in which we come together but must accept it as it is, its size, shape and situation (traffic noise, for example). Is loud playing possible without disturbing others? Such considerations will also play a part.

Orderliness makes a room pleasant and 'comprehensible' – we can take everything in. Beaters of various sizes stored in separate baskets; small objects such as bell sprays or woodblocks ordered into interesting, well-made boxes. Space might also be found for a large basket – a treasure trove of sundry objects for the children to rummage in, to explore and experiment. A stand on which the children can hang things is very useful; it is a meeting-point too. There should be space to move around in, the middle of the room generally left free for activities. One or two instruments set up in the middle stimulate the children into action. This 'middle' need not be determined by the symmetry of the room but by the group, and the therapist will inevitably consider in advance where in the room certain activities will work best.

The young therapist is justifiably nervous if *too much* material is immediately available to the children (if there are no storage cupboards in the room, for example). He is worried that the children will be tempted to use everything at the same time as this would make gestalt impossible. We must strive for an orderly, relative fullness that animates and fascinates without the negative effects of over-excitement.

VI Language

59

Language: when we speak, write or think we are using language. But language is at the same time more than just speaking, writing or thinking. Language is as much a part of living as physical movement: it is motion of the inner self. We can communicate with each other without any language at all; with a mass of words only confuse. A single word can convey more than a whole sentence while a sigh is in itself an expression of *something*. Things, whether natural or man-made, have their own form of language; 'That really *says* something to me'. Surprise, joy or pain can render us speechless.

Language is the dwelling-place of existence. Mankind lives within its walls.

Martin Heidegger

Any encounter only really comes to life in dialogue.

F.J.J. Buytendijk

One language stands above all others – and it requires no words.

C.J. Burkhardt

In Music Therapy:

Today's view of music therapy as a form of non-verbal language is certainly correct. However, and especially in therapy with adults, it should not be exclusively so. A verbal 'working-out' of what has been 'said' musically should complete the process. In therapy with children, on the other hand, a different use of language is called for. A rational, instructive style ('Look, let's do it like this', 'Wouldn't you really like to join in?') gives way to a rhythmic, more 'exhalted' (poetic even) use of language with which the therapist (taking care not to become unnaturally affected) responds to and encourages the child.

(. . . dialogue . . .) only a sigh perhaps, a quick intake of breath, a scarcely audible mumble or a catch of breath.

F.J.J. Buytendijk

Example: With a group of three or four children entering the room uncertainly, the therapist could perhaps sing: 'We're coming, we're coming, now we're here', improvising as the children find their places on the rugs provided. There each child might find a pair of claves, a non-verbal stimulus. Without speaking, the therapist starts to play her claves – or perhaps a child beats her to it – and the conditions for inventiveness, responding to each other as in a Rondo, or even just placing the claves to form a pattern will all play a meaningful part.

Putting ideas into words during a session can be important. The word 'background' arose in a session with three behaviourally disturbed, normally intelligent boys. One boy, sitting outside the main group, happened to be playing the bass xylophone just as a second boy wanted to play a solo. The therapist provided a small comment to calm things down: 'L is playing in the background'. The word, casually thrown in, was taken up by the second boy. 'You play the main part and I'll do the background', he said to the therapist. He had used the word 'background' to complement the 'main part' (German: Hintergrund/Vordergrund) and had associated the terms with quiet and loud so providing material for future sessions.

Another example: A melody of just four notes created by a child on a disarranged instrument led to this situation. By 'disarranged' we mean an instrument such as a xylophone where the bars have been removed and replaced at random. If we play a 'scale' on such an instrument we discover surprising combinations of pitches. Thomas stuck to just four notes, repeating them over and over again, and said: 'This is the evening'.

In the next session he looked for his 'evening' again and was just as enraptured by it as before, saying: 'If we hadn't disarranged it we would never have discovered this'. Six months later, when he was no longer attending therapy sessions, we were talking on the telephone when he suddenly said, 'do you still remember the "evening"?' Words can imprint themselves that deeply.

60

Rhyme: an identity of sound between two words where there is also a sense association. For a discussion of all the various forms of rhyme see OMT p.43 (Dante: *Divine Comedy*).

In Music Therapy:
The ability to appreciate rhyme is a diagnostic criterion. Without outside help, severely mentally handicapped children have no awareness of rhyme, no feeling for it. They can, however, be led to an appreciation of it which in turn can help to broaden their awareness in general. *The added element – sound – that rhyme brings enriches language and extends its possible uses.* It can also help in gaining and holding a child's attention. A behaviourally disturbed child, however, often demonstrates an unnaturally over-developed fascination for rhyme – 'rhyme-itis' (especially around the age of seven or eight). This condition, which certainly results from a certain isolation, itself isolates the child even more. He entangles himself to the extent that normal dialogue with others becomes impossible. Progress can, however, be achieved if more than one child with this condition are together in a group session. The therapist can, by playing on the 'rhyme-itis' of one child and stimulating the other children to do the same, motivate him to assert himself socially. This can help him overcome his compulsion.

61

Consonants: together with vowels are the building elements of language. Vowels are 'housed' inside consonants, so to speak, they are confined within them but can break out: seat-sea, treat-tree. Consonants are dynamic sounds that determine the shape of a language. The fact that some languages are dominated by consonants and others by vowels can provide much food for thought. (NB. The phenomenon in German of a 'word-body' in which various 'hearts' can be implanted: lEben lAben lIeben lOben.) As with rhyme, pertinent associations of meaning enrich the wordplay.

In Music Therapy:

The importance of language in the Orff-Schulwerk leads in turn to the large part played by phonetics in the Orff Music Therapy. Consonants, abundantly used and over-emphasised, can be recommended (see **ISO-Principle** – No.67) in work with the behaviourally disturbed (see OMT pp.38-44). Vowels are effective with shy and tentative children, a progression from vowel-dominated to consonant-dominated language with blind children. One blind child, Antonia, demonstrated the latter. Her first word was an expressionless 'amalgafei'. Later, less inhibited and accompanying herself on a drum, she came out with 'ssamala, ssamala erm'. The therapist developed this into 'ssamala, zerm' and Antonia understood and was delighted. She developed into a quite normal-speaking child.

A child I considered autistic, who didn't speak, was fascinated by a chain (German – 'KETTE') and this was his first word. But he swallowed the vowel and it came out as 'KTT'. Similarly, an English-speaking autistic child said 'CK' instead of 'CAKE'.

62

Vowels: the musical elements of language, the resonant resting-points within its flow. The various vowel-sounds give a language its undulating elasticity. The vocalic climaxes stimulate our sensitivity to the ebb and flow in the stream of language. In this sense, consonants *contain* the flow of language, form the banks.

In Music Therapy:

Depending on the type of handicap, it can be an important consideration in the therapy whether to lay more emphasis (with the aid of the appropriate musical instruments) on the vowels or on the consonants. In this context the lingering sonority of metallophones, glockenspiels, gongs and cymbals can be seen as vocalic. Consonantal, on the other hand, are the shortlived sounds made on the various woodblocks or the xylophone that simply *demand* to be repeated and excite physical involvement. In between these extremes lie those sounds made by beating membranic instruments which, depending on just how they are struck, can aid work either with vowels or with consonants. With activities such as these, children capable of normal speech can be given a new impulse in their use of language and possible shortcomings at school rectified.

Clearly, any simple classification of *all* sounds (vocalic/conson-antal) will not be possible, but even in cases of doubt we can ascertain a tendency of a particular sound to one side or the other: for example, sounds made on stone, glass, shells or stretched strings.

A very behaviourally disturbed boy was fascinated by the sound he made by striking on marble. He repeated it time and again until confident of it and then asked me: 'How does the sound get in there?'

63

Mutism: a refusal to speak which can be either partial (for example, only when not at home) or total (not at home either).

In Music Therapy:

A non-verbal child's reaction to an experience is silence. Ques-tions are ignored and he finds, of his own accord, no impetus to express himself verbally. To maintain this 'role', so to speak, the child is apathetic and avoids showing any interest that might compromise him emotionally. A non-verbal child usually carries himself well. He is likely to roam about in the room, avoiding eye contact and ignoring all calls to participate. In spite of this, the therapist *should* challenge him to respond, and make (not too demanding) instruments available in an attempt to energize his interest, to 'load' his curiosity to the extent that an inner compulsion forces him to do *something*, to touch *something*. The therapist could play a little on this or that instrument, stressing rhythm rather than melody, but not totally ignoring the latter as the non-verbal child will do. When, at last, the child feels compelled to act, he will casually begin to play on something – usually something wooden, the leg of a chair, a table, the wooden floor. He will not risk, for example, the reverberant metallophone for he cannot abandon himself to the sound. Any such submission would force him to reveal more of himself.

Examples: Birgit, a six-year-old girl, behaved in this way for several weeks until one day she surprised the therapist with the words: 'That's the middle'. She was standing in front of a xylophone and playing the middle note. A beginning! Although the words were scarcely audible, as if she was trying something out, this was a turning-point. 'Then we can take out the middle and we've got *here* and *there*.' (The therapist played the c – a to the left of the middle and the higher c – a to the right.) Now there was common ground to work on, a reaction that could be developed further . . . 'or should we *just* play the middle note?' . . . 'where can we find the middle note on this metallophone?' . . . seemingly unintentionally challenging the child: as if, in fact, the therapist is discovering something too . . . 'look! we *both* find the middle note here!' Being careful not to overdo it, the therapist 'worked' this initial material; it was, after all, all she had. Her progress was by no means smooth but after several sessions Birgit *did* develop her speech capabilities considerably.

Whenever she saw me at the Kinderzentrum she asked, 'When do we have music therapy again?', without any difficulty at all. She was able to go to a normal school.

Sybille, a remarkable pretty girl of seven, also just wandered about the room avoiding any eye-contact. Her arms were full with two big dolls which made it impossible for her to touch anything. Then the therapist spun a rotating drum and said, 'Why don't you let the dolls ride on the round-about?' The idea intrigued her. She put the dolls on the drum and played on it as it turned – and her facial expression softened! (When a non-verbal child's facial expression is not showing indifference it often shows complete mental absorption. Frowning and knitting his brows, as if occupied with a difficult problem, the child is warning 'do not disturb'.) She then sat down at the xylophone close by and for a little while played along . . . 'da wo ich bin, da wo ich nicht bin' (here I am, here I'm not). Suddenly she began a song she knew well but finished the line in her own way: 'Ich bin da, du bist da, wackawackawa, wackawawa' (I'm here, you're here, mamamamamere, mamameremere) . . . a playful rhythmic accompaniment out of her present frame of mind. That done she stood up; she had accomplished something! One could detect, however, from the new way she carried herself, that she would welcome a new challenge.

64

Echolalia: simple repetition of one's own words or somebody else's. The to and fro of normal conversation is missing. A verbal 'walking on the spot'.

In Music Therapy:

Blind children often demonstrate echolalia. One could say it is more or less normal for them: the blind child asserts himself and what he has said by repetition. It can easily occur up to five times in succession. Echolalia compensates the blind child for the normal corroboration through eye-contact with one's *vis-à-vis* that he lacks. When it occurs the child is simply not yet ready for normal conversation. One should accept the echolalia and not try to drive it out. And one should be careful not to make an over-hasty negative prognosis. In his own good time, the blind child will shrug off this necessity to repeat everything and be able to reply normally. It can even happen that the blind child compels the therapist to repeat his (the child's) words. This confirmation is a moment of triumph for the child!

Example: I was able to observe the whole process with Antonia. At first this blind girl said nothing at all, then she would only whisper until, finally, she spoke loud enough to be understood – but always with repetitions . . . 'That's a drumstick, that's a drumstick, that's a soft drumstick, that's a soft drumstick'. The therapist's question 'do you want a drumstick?' received the reply 'do you want a drumstick' and so on. I left the child to her compulsion without realizing at the time just how easily she would eventually overcome it.

When a mentally handicapped child demonstrates echolalia, this at least shows that language has been apprehended, if only on the phonetic level. The repetitions too may be only phonetic. Nevertheless they may serve to drive home the sounds to the extent that eventually words can be understood. If the child always repeats only one word, the therapist must be careful not to reply in one-word sentences but should continue to use full sentences. In most cases, the child repeats the therapist's last word: 'do you want the ball?' – 'ball', 'do you want the red ball?' – eventually the child will repeat 'red ball'. One could almost say that such children build their sentences from back to front.

65

Yes—No responses: the child can react to everything only with affirmation/assent or with negation/rejection respectively. The reaction is rarely spontaneous, neither is it an expression of a genuine opinion or present state of mind.

In Music Therapy:

'Yes-responders' are children who do not want to attract attention to themselves or offer any form of resistance. Either they have no opinion of their own or cannot trust themselves to form one. The 'No-response' is a defence-mechanism similar to the 'Yes-response', but more negative. In both cases the response 'I can't, I don't want to', has become so habitual as to be effectively reflex. This can be as a result of anxiety, of expediency or of a negative social awareness. With 'Yes-responders' the aim must be to provoke some form of opposition and to trace the reasons for such passivity. 'No-responders' should be approached less directly: by means of peripheral activities the therapist encourages them to take an interest and notes just when and in response to what the first 'Yes' is achieved.

The moment when a 'Yes-responder' manages a 'No' is just as important. If the child understands language, the therapist could ask questions where the only possible answer is 'no' and to answer with 'yes' would just make nonsense. 'Is it snowing today?' – 'Yes', 'is the sun shining?' – 'Yes' . . . 'No!'. The child has to laugh! 'Yes-responders' are often unsure of themselves physically as well; their arms firmly at their sides they gesticulate very little. So it was in the case of the fourteen-year-old Paula – nothing but a whispered 'yes', appropriate or not. Relaxed, swaying movement- and dance-games with a partner helped. Facing each other and moving alternately to the left and the right (not mirror-image but each to her own left and right) each may be pointing in a different direction but neither is 'wrong', this helped her to more self-assertion. At home Paula was aggressive, always trying to have her own way; in unfamiliar surroundings, and also at school, she would always show this indecisive, affirmative behaviour, contrary to her true disposition. Her playing on pitched instruments was very compressed, mostly in seconds,

and the therapist encouraged her to broaden it and also to play loudly. She managed at best a *mezzo-forte*. Her 'Yes-es' were spoken in a very high voice but this gradually became lower; it was possible to stimulate her to more individuality in her playing and she was noticeably happier and more relaxed. In front of visitors to the institute however, something we thought she could cope with, she was once more reserved and restrained, a 'no' or any other word but 'yes' trickling out only with great difficulty.

VII Communication

66

Play implies interplay, there must be give and take.

Marshall McLuhan

Communication: mutual participation, also sharing. Hidden in the word is the Latin 'munus' meaning, on the one hand, obligation or duty, but on the other hand, gift or offering. Communication is made possible only by effort in a spirit of giving.

In Music Therapy:

Communication ought to be achieved during a session. It encourages the children to listen to one another and promotes mutual give and take. So does play. In play, therefore, children can discover and practise communication. Practice is essential, for communication is only acquired through effort – it does not 'fall into one's lap'.

67

ISO-Principle: derived from the Greek word 'isos' = the same, similar (iso-theos = godlike).

In Music Therapy:

The therapist acts in accordance with the ISO-Principle when his reactions to a child are determined by the child's behaviour in the sense of being a mirror-image of that behaviour. Even if the child's behaviour is 'disturbed' (or clearly not 'normal'), the therapist offers no contrary responses; his ISO-responses may be neutral but not antithetical. He will not, for example, offer a quiet instrument or suggest a calm activity to a child who is being noisy and rowdy; he will not force himself or an activity on a shy child. He knows that, in the course of the therapy, the child will recognize for himself negative traits and eventually overcome them. The therapist's immediate concern, however, is with the 'here and now'!

. . . to put their charges to sleep, they (the nurses) do not resort to stillness or quietude. On the contrary, they employ movement, and constantly rock the children in their arms. Neither do they remain silent as they do so, but sing them little songs and virtually make music with them.

Plato

In the world of medicine, homoeopathy is a comparable concept to ISO. The homoeopathist administers relevant doses of the same substances that caused the illness, treating like with like (one could almost term this method provocative), while allopathic medicine makes use of foreign substances.

The Ancient Greeks also distinguished between homoeopathy and allopathy as Plato's poetic description of sending a baby to sleep demonstrates: inner commotion is overcome by means of physical movement, like cures like.

Traditional lullabies are for this reason usually lively songs. In the well-known German lullaby *Schlaf, Kindlein, schlaf*, the long, calming 'a'-sounds (schlaaaf) are followed by vigorous consonants: schütteln, Bäumelein, fällt, 'Die Mutter schüttelt's Bäumelein, da fällt herab ein Träumelein,' (*The mother shakes the little tree until a dream falls down out of it*) in a lively quaver rhythm (see also the comments on the lengths of melodies in No.52). Among the English lullabies, the dance-like, dotted rhythms in *Rock-a-bye baby* offer another good example.

To complement my repeated references to ISO in the course of the text, here are two further examples.

Towards the end of a session – it was the ninth – a five-year-old boy whom I had judged to be autistic, suddenly started to scream wildly (the boy is small enough to be mistaken for a two-year-old, understands speech but does not speak himself; he cannot develop a relationship to objects but is always laden with 'security-toys'). Occasionally he would make a sound and showed an increasing tendency to express himself in sounds; recently his first, intelligible word was 'haben' (have) – was he demanding something for himself?

He had been participating in the session: he had played the lyre a little and made the beads in the drum move about; he had stretched out on the floor (the position he always took up when he felt at ease) to listen to the others – his mien showed that he was feeling confident and untroubled and he was taking, for him, an unusually active part in the session. Then he noticed a cassette-recorder that I had been using in a previous session and not yet put away, and he broke out into a panic. I have not been able to discover what associations he made with the recorder that caused this reaction; perhaps he was thinking of a similar recorder at home. (This was his second state of panic in the session: earlier he had been horrified at discovering my chains (see No.42) 'open'. He had often handled them in the past – they had become a means of establishing initial contact – and was now shocked at finding them not 'closed'; he almost found words for his feelings! My reactions enabled him eventually to be calm again.) Now, for a second time, he threw himself down, gesturing wildly and screaming; it was impossible to pacify him. This was the first time I had encountered such panic with this child. I reached for the nearest object which happened to be a children's harp, an instrument we rarely use because the frame is too weak to support the strings, leaving many of them loose and out of tune. In the present situation this was, if anything, an advantage! Loudly, I played all the strings at once, screaming with him in support. The effect on him was as dramatic as the sudden and total change we often observe in the weather: from overcast hailstorms to calm, sunny skies. He beamed at me as if to say 'that was just right', stopped screaming and busied himself a little with the harp. Indeed he let himself be interested in an activity longer than usual and left the session a contented child. ISO!

Another example: A clever nine-year-old boy with dyslexia is sent to music therapy. He comes in, sits down and looks totally disinterested. He just doesn't care. This completely indifferent, dismissive attitude was something new to me: children usually either express themselves verbally in a negative way or make a lot of noise; or one senses that they are frightened or uncomfortable – but this nothingness! What was I to do? I asked a few neutral-sounding questions but he only shrugged his shoulders. Between us stood a xylophone and, as if I was only amusing myself, I started to play it. As I did so I casually asked, 'Do you know this one?' He shrugged his shoulders again. I played a glissando up and down the instrument as a challenge, at the same time, however, saying indifferently, 'You could do this too, you know'. And he really did it, producing a much more intensive glissando than mine. I told him so. I then said that that was a dash but one could also make a full-stop which I did by playing a single note. His mien showed no interest at all but he played a full-stop too, although he seemed to be saying, 'Well, if it makes you happy!'

Ignoring him completely, I stood up and played dashes and full-stops on the other instruments in the room. He stood up too and played intensively on the same instruments and to the same extent that I had; he was imitating and not being provocative but his mien remained unchanged still. Again I told him how good I found his playing. The session was a short, introductory one and at the end I said, 'The next session won't be for another two weeks'. He replied, 'Oh! In two weeks' time then!' When he arrived two weeks later his mien was transformed, bright and clear. During the session he did nothing very constructive, mostly throwing up and catching a beater, watching himself in the mirror as he did so, but he stayed the whole hour and at the end said, 'In another two weeks then?' I was able to tell him, 'No, next week' and he was clearly pleased. The third session has not yet taken place.

As I have described earlier (see also the OMT), a child must be won over in the very first session. He must leave the session thinking, 'I hope I'll be back soon'.

68

Peripheral: oblique, roundabout approach to a child.

In Music Therapy:

In therapy this concept refers to the possibility of indirectly challenging a child. Avoiding direct visual contact and giving no direct or concrete suggestions one establishes contact and seemingly accidentally captures the child's interest. Sensitive children react well to this peripheral approach as it leaves them sufficient 'space' in which to work. At the same time the child feels himself sucked in, looking for the 'central-point' that is missing. Mentally handicapped children, on the other hand, should be approached directly as should loud and unruly behaviourally disturbed children (see **ISO-Principle** – No.67).

Boys especially show a tendency to play an instrument 'into the wall'. With their backs to the centre of the room and the limits of the space – the wall – in full view, they feel sure of themselves and their playing is uninhibited. They find face-to-face confrontation too direct.

69

Patience: a 'virtue' that can only be acquired and which the therapist *must* acquire. The ability to endure conditions felt to be irritating, disagreeable or even offensive for which we have no immediate remedy.

In Music Therapy:

Time is not necessarily an element of patience (enduring something for a certain length of time) and neither should patience be understood in a passive sense ('putting up with something'). A split-second reaction can reveal whether patience is really present; did my actions, my mien and my tone of voice demonstrate complete patience with *no trace* of impatience?

The 'emptiness' (see No.55) of the therapist is often required to produce instantaneously a helping word, tone or idea from his reservoir of patience – an extremely *active* process. In this sense, patience implies not suffering under, but *sharing* a load. Genuine communication is not possible without tolerance and patience, without giving others what we are able to give and accepting only their problems in return. Being unaffected or untouched by such problems – 'immune' – would be a fundamentally anti-therapeutic attitude.

70

Responsibility: can be assumed for a person, object or idea. If we take seriously the concept 'response' contained in the word, then the person or object reacts to this concern, is aware that a 'question' is put in order to provoke an 'answer'. In therapy our actions will always have a determining influence on the echo that results, on the response.

In Music Therapy:

Responsibility is an element in every therapeutic encounter. The therapist accepts the situation as it is and not as he would like it to be; he accepts the child as he is. The child should sense this responsibility and, for his part, learn to appreciate limits: just how far can I go with this instrument, how loudly can I play, what treatment will this object allow? The therapist must discover what motivates a child to play loudly or unbearably aggressively: is intervention justifiable or would it be irresponsible? Mutual tolerance is essential and leads to a healthy understanding of the meaning of responsibility.

Example: One nine-year-old girl, a foster child diagnosed as mentally handicapped, played the instruments almost unbearably loudly and violently – louder and more violently than any child before her. As she went around the room she played on every available instrument: three kettle-drums, the bass drum, three xylophones, three metallophones, four glockenspiels, woodblocks, bongos, gong, two cymbals, all played violently and without interruption. She went around a second time taking with her various different beaters and at each instrument decided quickly and confidently which beater was the most suitable. She carried herself well, her head held high, 'crowning' herself occasionally with a basket. In a later session I suggested I turn my back to her and try to guess which instrument she was playing. She agreed to this. She took her time choosing an instrument, already an element of self-restraint. As she did so I occupied myself by playing on the 'tree' (see **Order** – No.27) that stood in my corner. She reacted immediately when I suddenly stopped playing and said (sang out) calmly 'mo-re' almost in a falling fifth.

I played on and again stopped – the same calm reaction followed. She was clearly capable of listening attentively to me and simultaneously considering which instrument she should play, commenting as she did so: 'this one perhaps', 'or this', 'or even this one'. Having chosen, she once more rained (mostly violent) blows on her instrument but, surprisingly, some strokes were quiet and gentle.

During the next session she heightened the tension by deliberately taking longer to decide – I was forbidden to look – and she collected together various similar-sounding instruments: her careful performance produced a profusion of soft, calm timbres.

Clearly, this girl was capable of learning, of deciding what to do and how. At first her voice had been almost frighteningly low and coarse but now it developed more gentle modulations. She abandoned her one-word sentences and spoke in proper if not quite complete ones, and her gloomy, impenetrable expression brightened into a smile. Her therapy is still in progress and we confidently expect continued improvement in her speech, social awareness and her overall development.

71

Need: the onomatopoetically pleading 'nee' finds resolution in the terminal 'd'. Nu, nun (Latin 'nunc') – retraceable to its Indo-Germanic roots – has no resolving consonant.

In Music Therapy:

This isolation *must* be unlocked. It is especially noticeable in non-speaking children (mutism) and found in intensified form in autistic behaviour. Such complete isolation must be approached carefully. Bruno Bettelheim gives his book on autism the particularly suitable title *The Empty Fortress*: true need is found in this imprisoning isolation, no possibility of verbal communication, inner constriction and suppressed emotions. An 'O', the symbol for self-containment which itself implies seclusion, is compressed almost to a straight line, a balloon void of air. This need can and must be broken into with the warmth of our feelings and emotions whereby the person in need will, almost certainly, resist and rebuff our approaches.

In therapy, a refusal to play is a clear indication of this need. Children will avoid pleasantly resonant, reverberating instruments, such as the metallophone, in particular. They might retreat from intervals altogether and seek refuge in bare rhythmic phrases. If we try to imagine just how difficult it is for somebody who can speak not to do so, not to express himself, for any length of time, we can perhaps understand the plight of the permanently isolated whose

We can assume . . . that emotions are the motive power that provokes and animates dialogue.

René Spitz

88

thoughts and feelings are *always* directed inwards. Accumulated feelings and past experiences must be continually 'compressed' to make room for reactions to new events. For this reason, the therapist should on no account offer new material before the child is able to release some of the pressure within him into the outside world. The therapist's responsibility is to persevere until he discovers an 'outlet'.

72

Necessity: a concept implying an urgent and compelling challenge. If an action is 'necessary' it means, on the one hand, that there is no alternative course, and on the other, that the action is essential and unavoidable. It *will* bring about a change. If we are reluctant to do the necessary it is perhaps because of its associations with 'duty' or 'obligation'; in our work we are usually concerned with the spontaneous and the creative. In this sense, the presence of the word 'necessity' in our catalogue of therapeutic words is almost a provocation. But 'provocation' itself is a therapeutic necessity.

Example: . . . a seven-year-old boy severely retarded in his development. His perceptive abilities were good although he did not speak. His movements were also good although usually deliberately and ostentatiously slow; he was only quick when he avidly wanted something (chocolate, for example). This boy angrily rejected any assistance from me even if the task he had set himself was impossibly difficult for him. He had strong autistic tendencies which stopped him showing his true feelings.

Whenever he came into the room, he would quickly ascertain where the chains were or if they were there at all. If he found them he would proceed with the following long-drawn ritual. He removed the marbles from the Kugelturm (see **Structure** – No.40), divided them into three equal piles and then fetched the pieces of hose. (A piece about a meter long will produce an F if swung around moderately quickly. Swung harder, it will produce the third above (A) or even the fifth (C); swung slowly, the C a fourth below sounds.) Any swinging at all was too much effort for this boy! He slowly and conscientiously filled the hose with the marbles that he had laid ready. I pretended to be completely preoccupied with an instrument and deliberately avoided watching what he was doing: he did not seem to mind my playing. Having filled the pieces of hose (he could take as long as twenty minutes for this) he went carefully over to the Kugelturm and tried to feed the marbles into it from the hose, a look of the utmost concentration on his face. This was much too difficult for him but he rejected any help from me with an angry hiss and a tendency to try to bite. After several such unsuccessful attempts I stepped in forcefully, gripped his hand and helped steer the balls. His expression was transformed immediately from one of angry rejection to one of astonished, fascinated acceptance. After this, he never wanted to do it alone again but always asked me, with an imploring look, to help him.

For him too, the chains had been a starting point. He handled them almost reverently, lifting them up and letting them fall back into their jar, and growled threateningly at me if I tried to touch them. They provided the stimulus for his first spoken word: 'K(e)tt(e)' (chain). He pronounced the word without the vowels. Other words that he spoke of his own accord were 'nopal' (nochmal = again) and 'Halt'. He wanted to monopolize the hoops as well and defended them just as aggressively as the other objects. However, when one day I took them 'by force', his defence evaporated; he seemed relieved that I had at last dared to assert myself. Now we lifted the hoops together, moved them here and there, swung them from side to side. At last he was prepared to collaborate in an activity; he learnt several new words and left us after three months' therapy with a much greater readiness to accept both assistance and new challenges.

73

Acceptance: taking, receiving, is commonly understood to be a passive act. Its Latin root 'capere', means to take but also to select. The Greek word 'kapto' is even more active – to seize, grasp or snatch; also snatch at with the mouth, receive orally and understand. The Greek root thus indicates the oral nature of the initial phase of understanding.

In Music Therapy:

Acceptance in therapy is a two-way affair – the child accepts the therapist and the therapist accepts the child. The 'initiative' here remains the responsibility of the therapist: he will not pre-judge the child, not even allowing his diagnosis to prevent him confronting the child with a completely open mind. He will attempt to understand the child. This will often be a difficult and protracted undertaking during which the therapist will give the child free rein and allow him to act exactly as he wants to. It is enough for the therapist to be present, accompanying the child in what he does, side by side with him, facing him or backing him up. Quite unnecessary are permanent eye-contact or continued friendly, sympathetic, or encouraging smiles. The therapist should also avoid speaking unnaturally distinctly or with exaggeratedly quiet, reverent articulation. (It may seem paradoxical but children do not require that adults speak over-clearly in order to learn to speak clearly themselves. The example of a natural mode of speech, not unclearly of course but in a 'matter of fact' way and casually, with many repetitions, is enough.) The therapist must accept the inevitable shyness that most children naturally bring with them. With children who lack this sense of distance the therapist will attempt to erect a 'barrier' between himself and the child sitting opposite him. An instrument makes an ideal 'barrier'.

Example: A girl suffering from a progressive illness that had stunted her growth and considerably retarded her mental development (at six she gave the impression of a three-year-old) achieved clear speech through actions. At first she spoke only an occasional, unintelligible word. Acting out an idea such as 'sleeping' (she would be covered with a blanket and then 'woken up') caused her to say suddenly, 'tir-ed'. She wrapped chime bars in cloths and then unwrapped them again and said, 'nap-pies'. Her pronunciation was unnaturally exaggerated but she beamed as she heard her own voice. In a situation such as this – a beginning with a particular child – acceptance can mean that the therapist listens to the child, nods and smiles even if he has not understood or can only guess what has been said. Questioning the child – 'what did you say?' – would only silence him. I discovered that an over-eager colleague had tried too hard to maintain intense eye-contact with this child while speaking to her in an unnaturally clear voice. The result had been that the child immediately said and did *nothing* further. No amount of loving, encouraging looks can rectify such a situation. At the beginning this girl could hardly walk. In the course of a year's therapy she learnt to do so confidently and even showed signs of wanting to hop and jump. She loved it when we formed a circle out of various rugs and walked around this circle to a signal (a drumbeat perhaps) standing on one of the rugs when the signal stopped; a different signal meant we had to walk backwards and so on. She would also make the signals for her mother and me as we walked around the circle. We built up this complex in linear co-ordination: a) becoming aware of the path to follow, from rug to rug, b) comprehension of the complete 'scenario', walking around the whole circle, c) responding to a signal, d) registering when there was no signal and standing still.

It is often unclear to what extent a child accepts the therapist, but this is, at least at the beginning, of no importance. The therapist has no real need to know; it is enough to be sure that the child will return. There can be exceptions but in my opinion it is not even necessary to ask the child if he has enjoyed himself. A child with a strong personality can challenge or provoke the therapist. Looking for confirmation of his strengths he tries to measure himself against the therapist, wants to do everything better and so on. The therapist must avoid the temptation to compete with him!

Example: I was confronted once with a behaviourally disturbed boy of eight or nine who refused at first to come to therapy at all (a psychologist had recommended it) and certainly not 'to a woman'! He left the first session obviously pleased with himself. In later sessions he did all he could to disturb! In reality this permanent provocation was an attempt to gain my acceptance. Finally he brought me a present: it was something very useful that he had seen I did not have!

74

Authority: a difficult word nowadays, often misunderstood, variously used and abused. Authority exists and therefore can neither be denied nor wished away.

In Music Therapy:

An adult is and should be an authority (in his own way, a child is also an authority) that can react in different ways as the occasion demands, but cannot absent itself completely. There are therapeutic situations where a therapist will withdraw almost completely, where he will 'take a back seat' to such an extent that his presence is almost unnoticed. In group work especially, his contribution to the dynamism of the activities is switched almost to nil but it is not switched off altogether. At any moment a child or the group may require that the therapist abandons this 'neutral' position (see **Emptiness** – No.55) in order to sanction an activity, to settle a quarrel or to animate with new ideas.

Authoritarian, domineering behaviour, on the other hand, is unacceptable and harmful. The development and optimal use of authority is a fundamental demand made on a therapist (pedagogue) but one that requires a lifelong learning-process.

75

Therapist: the Greek origins of the word show us the way: servant, companion, healer.

In Music Therapy:

Music therapy demands of the therapist a variety of personal characteristics, some of which even seem to contradict each other – calm *and* lively, or cautious *and* spontaneous. He should prepare each encounter in advance but be ready for and sensitive to different requirements that the children might have, and not stand in their way; helpful and flexible. Sensitive but at the same time thick-skinned and impervious to all hostile shafts hurled at him. This aspect of his work – not being hurt – is one that he must work on especially. He is likely to be most deeply affected by the miserable condition of some of his patients but he must learn to overcome this. If he is at first so overcome by their problems and handicaps that he thinks he cannot go on, he will later develop a more neutral position. He has to, for this helps nobody. It is important, however, for him to have lived through this initial suffering.

The therapist is an axis around which the child revolves. No matter how far the child distances himself, he is always aware that he can rely on this firm connection to a focal point: he is not lost. Another implication of this image of an axis, namely that the therapist does not come too near to the child, is also important for the success of the therapy. The therapist must always be aware that he is a mediator. Through him the child may achieve independence and develop interests whether for other people or for objects. If the therapist is successful, then, when the child no longer needs therapy, the break with him will not be traumatic. The binding axis is casually lengthened in time and space leaving an unforgotten but uncomplicated and painless bond. The therapy must never become an exercise in self-awareness training for the therapist; the object of the situation must never, even in part, be his experience. Paradoxically, this necessary self-restraint itself *is* training and promotes greater self-awareness.

76

Cantus-memoria-meditatio: literally song, memory, reflection (see OMT pp.63-66).

In Music Therapy:

'Cantus', song, singing is meant in the widest possible sense: the entire being expressing itself, proclaiming its existence – a look, sigh, speech, movement all saying 'here I am, now! and how wonderful it is'. Such an experience remains in and indeed fosters the memory, it becomes a part of us, a treasured possession. It provides the nourishment for meditatio too, is a foretaste of the next encounter: if . . . then . . . depending on the capabilities and capacities of the individual. The most severely handicapped child will, at the latest on re-entering the therapy room, experience *some* memoria and meditatio – remembering what was and wanting more. Many mothers speak of their child's reactions on the way to the therapy: 'When he realizes where we are going, he's always happy and excited!'

The use of the word 'cantus' in Italian is especially extensive: canta il gallo = the cock *crows*, canta il usignolo = the nightingale *sings*, canta la cicala = the cricket *chirps*; far cantare = to make somebody talk; the expression 'canta che ti passa' = 'everything will be all right' (will sing again). As the tangled, tragic inevitability of Oedipus becomes apparent, the chorus says (in Hölderlin's translation): 'What should I sing?' The situation is hopeless if one can no longer 'sing'; endless possibilities are open to the child that can experience cantus!

A talented, six-year-old boy with enormous problems in communicating with others said, when he came into the room for the first time, 'This is just right for me, I can sing here!' (After four sessions, he has not yet sung a single tone in the literal sense of the word!)

He drew the picture 'A with a guitar' (see the illustration in No.5). The fact that he was allowed to keep a guitar with him during the session and 'play' it too (his mother who was present, said, 'He always wants to have a guitar but he can't even play it!'), and that what he 'played' on it here was 'acceptable', made such a strong impression on him that he brought me this drawing on his next visit. It is drawn completely in red.

Cantus *is* a moment of 'elevation'.

77

Response: a word received as a reaction to what one has said. A response can be appropriate to the initial statement. It might encourage further discussion, or it might abruptly end it. The possibility of an unexpected response can never be ruled out; the reaction of a *vis-à-vis*, an 'opposite', will always be more or less 'anti'.

In Music Therapy:

We need a response, *any* response, with which to work – even uncomfortable, difficult responses are welcome. After all, therapy means acceptance, helping, 'going along with'. The response determines the nature of the therapy. A monologue from a therapist brings nothing. Dialogue produces material that can be taken up and 'worked'.

The circle must be completed – perception, ISO-treatment, provocation, acceptance of the response. The response shows us what the therapy has achieved, the therapy culminates in the response.

A response is possible on various, different levels; a delayed response is also possible. It can be a look, a smile, a turning towards or away. It can be a prompt imitation of a rhythm or spontaneous glissandi. Defiance or incapacity might delay a response until the next opportunity arrives – then it comes as a surprise to the therapist.

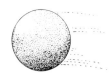

The therapist *must* elicit a response from the child to initiate a to and fro – playful, casual, rash, precise, logical – anything is possible. The therapist's unfailing, perceptive receptiveness (to the extent of his abilities) accepts the response, assimilates it, ponders and evaluates it.

We are permanently in motion (life *means* motion) and must be prepared to accept the responsibility for every moment in our lives. Every moment requires of us the full extent of our abilities and our individuality to judge the necessary response: still or active, restrained or voluminous, strict or indulgent. A response is a gift.

Index

Included in this index are:

1. the 77 concepts (in bold print)
2. handicaps described in the text
3. children discussed, classified according to age and age-related generalizations
4. instruments used in the therapy
5. some additional concepts